HOW TO RESTORE ANTIQUE FURNITURE

What-not.

How to Restore
ANTIQUE
FURNITURE

Colin
Holcombe

The Crowood Press

First published in 1996 by
The Crowood Press Ltd
Ramsbury, Marlborough
Wiltshire SN8 2HR

British Library Cataloguing in Publication Data

A catalogue record for this book is available from the British Library.

ISBN 1 86126 008 3

Acknowledgements

I would like to acknowledge the help of Dave Hartnell for his expertise with a camera. Photographs by kind permission of Balmuir House Antiques, Breakspeare Antiques and Day Antiques (all of Tetbury in Gloucestershire).

Line-drawings by the author and David Fisher

Typeset by Phoenix Typesetting, Ilkley, West Yorkshire
Printed and bound in Great Britain by BPC Books Ltd, Aylesbury

CONTENTS

CONTENTS

Preface

I learnt the basics of woodwork at Bishopston Secondary Modern School in Bristol, under the watchful eye of an old-style woodwork teacher by the name of Mr Hody. I was preparing for my O level examinations when the opportunity arose to start an apprenticeship as an antique restorer with a firm of antique dealers in Bristol called Hall and Rohan. They were not only one of the biggest antique dealers in Bristol at the time but they also had a huge stock of furniture that they kept for theatre hire. This meant that there was a large amount of furniture constantly being broken and on which an apprentice could be let loose. I served a five-year apprenticeship with them, under an Englishman who was also a semi-professional entertainer and taught me magic and got me into the Bristol Society of Magic, and an Italian restorer called Carlo Perona. I survived nine years working with Carlo, who taught me most of what I know about both antique restoration and life. Carlo's philosophy was to respect everyone, unless they gave you good reason not to, and to make the best of whatever situation you found yourself in.

I use the word survive to describe the time I spent with him because as well as a brilliant restorer, he was also a somewhat accident-prone inventor. At one time we used to solder our own bandsaw blades if they broke, using a gas gun with two inlets and a pair of foot bellows. One inlet on the gun was connected to a gas supply and the other to the bellows: Carlo would turn on and light the gas and I would work the bellows. This method produced a good flame but required two people. Carlo one day decided that it would be more efficient to use a cylinder vacuum cleaner switched to blow, rather than the foot bellows. This did indeed achieve the desired result, but on one memorable occasion Carlo had turned on the gas as usual but was having trouble with his lighter. Calling me over for some matches he did not realize that the gas was not just coming out of the end of the gun, but was going back down the air inlet and filling up the vacuum cleaner. The gas was eventually lit but the explosion that resulted from turning on the vacuum cleaner had to be experienced; it cannot be described. We were both fortunate that the ends of the vacuum cleaner were only held on by small grub screws, as the force of the explosion was enough to blow them to opposite ends of the workshop.

After nine happy years with Hall and Rohan, I started work for a small firm making pine furniture. Unfortunately the firm did not stay in business very long and I found myself on the dole, and it seemed that the best solution to our problems was for me to go into business for myself. During my first year in business I was approached by an adult education authority to teach restoration and French polishing at nightschool, and it was then that people started asking me why I didn't write a book on the subject. I used to write information sheets for the class, and this got me started, but everything had to be written in long hand. It was not until we bought a computer and word processor that I really had the time and means to produce this book.

I was fortunate to have had a tutor like Carlo, who had a wealth of knowledge and was willing to pass it on. If Carlo had not been there, it would have been very helpful to have had a book like this to fall back on. I suggest you keep it close by your workbench.

Introduction

I started my apprenticeship as an antique furniture restorer with Hall and Rohan of the Mall in Bristol, in 1963 at the age of fifteen. Since that time I have seen many changes in the world of antiques – even in what is regarded as antique. In 1963 no antique shop of any quality would carry anything in its stock that was made after 1830. Indeed, Victorian furniture was our principal source of good timber and one of my jobs as the apprentice was to carefully dismantle any such furniture that came our way and make sure it found a home in the wood store. I am horrified when I remember the beautiful pieces of superb Victorian furniture – extending dining tables in particular – which were broken up to be used to restore earlier items. One of the main problems facing today's restorer is where to acquire good timber for restoration. The extending tables that we bought then for five or ten pounds, depending on the number of leaves, would today fetch four-figure sums. Thankfully, Victorian furniture has now acquired the status that it so richly deserves. Good-quality Victorian furniture is probably some of the best ever made. Great care was taken in the selection and treatment of the materials and great skill was employed in its manufacture. It is also a fact, of course, that the Victorian cabinet-maker had the advantage of improved tools and machinery over his predecessors. What a shame that so much of it is now lost to us, and how important that what remains should be cherished and preserved.

Another of the changes I have witnessed over my years in the trade is in the number and type of people who furnish with antiques. In 1963 most of the people we saw at the restoration workshop came from upper- or upper-middle-class backgrounds and had houses in the country. Now we get all types of people from all kinds of backgrounds, and even young people setting up home for the first time see the benefits of buying older furniture to start with. They know that they can often buy Victorian or Edwardian furniture more cheaply than they can buy new, and that later, if they want to change it, they will probably be able to get their money back or even make a modest profit. That would certainly not be the case if they bought new.

With the increasing numbers of people interested in antiques and the ever-decreasing stock of antiques, it is no surprise that restorers are now being asked to work on furniture manufactured in the 1920s and even the 1930s. It is also no surprise that the number of restorers has increased to meet this demand. There has, too, over the years been an increase in the number of people, both men and women, who have acquired woodworking skills and who feel that, with the right guidance, they could carry out some repairs themselves. For almost twenty years now I have run an adult evening class teaching furniture restoration and French polishing. Every year I am asked the same question: 'Is there a good book on the market that I could recommend?' Not a book that just goes through three or four projects, but a book that can be used much the same as a car mechanic would use a workshop manual. Well, now I can tell them: 'Yes, here it is.'

Enough about the antique trade and the people who buy antiques. What about restoration itself? Which of these three dictionary definitions would you consider most appropriate when we are talking about antique furniture?

Restore. To give back, to bring back into existence or use, to put back into a former or original unimpaired state.

Renovate. To restore to a former or improved state (for example by cleaning, repairing or rebuilding).

Repair. To restore by replacing a part or putting together what is torn or broken, to restore to a sound or healthy state, to remedy.

In truth, none of them quite fits the bill. Restoration and renovation both imply to me that we put the furniture back into its original pristine condition, and repairing somehow suggests that it would be all right to use plywood on table tops or to repair broken legs with metal brackets; both these things would be wrong. What we should or should not do when restoring antique furniture is a difficult question to answer, because it depends on a number of different things. If the piece in question is to be in regular use, then it has to be in a good enough state of repair to withstand being constantly handled. On the other hand, if it is to live out its time in a museum with a rope around it so that nobody can touch or sit on it, it need only look the part. Each case has to be considered on its merits.

It would be wrong to remove every mark or dent in a piece of furniture, and certainly wrong to remove all trace of wear and ageing, which would be necessary to restore it to its original unimpaired state.

Neither would we want to leave it with loose joints or lifting veneer, if it is to be used. Compromise, then, would seem to be the most sensible course of action. Do what is necessary to preserve the piece, depending on how much use it will have. We must be careful not to over-restore – we may want to take away some of the ravages of age, but we do not want to remove all signs. The smooth rounding of edges and the warm patina of long-polished surfaces are all part of what makes antiques desirable – these things are what set them apart from the new. They are the signature of its history and must be preserved, not removed. Some things are certain, however: if a piece is to be furnished with, loose joints must be reglued, broken legs and rails must be repaired, lifting veneer must be relaid and worn drawer runners must, if the drawer is to be used, be replaced. All, of course, must be done with care, knowledge and attention to detail, and preserving the piece's 'signature' of its history. Some of the decisions that are involved will be cut and dried, others will not be so easy. Should it be repolished? Should the small piece of missing veneer be replaced? Should the split in the top be repaired? In my opinion, antique furniture should be used and should look attractive and cared for. If this means that missing pieces have to be replaced or the item repolished, then, so long as the repairs are carried out with proper regard for the piece and by someone with the necessary skill and knowledge, these things are acceptable.

Now the subject of money rears its ugly head. Will having a piece restored affect its value? Yes, of course it will, but not always adversely. For example, if you have a piece of antique furniture in original condition which has survived the years without the need for repair or repolishing, this piece is both important and desirable. At auction it would realize more money than a similar piece which had been restored. On the other hand, the restored piece, if the restoration has been well done, will realize more than if it had been offered in a poor state of repair. In the end, you have to make up your own mind as to what should or should not be done. But what makes a good repair rather than a bad one? Well, ideally any restoration should be undetected; in many cases this is possible, but in others some sign of the restoration is inevitable. In these cases it is important that the restoration be carried out unobtrusively and with no attempt to alter or improve the piece in any way. Wherever possible, the same materials as the original should be used and if anything has to be replaced, this should be kept to an absolute minimum. It is my hope that this book will be useful in helping you make the correct decisions.

one

A Brief History of English Furniture Construction

English furniture of the sixteenth century consisted mainly of the chest, which would in many houses have served as a seat and a table, as well as a receptacle for the household's possessions. Richer households may have owned a table, stool or even in some cases a chair. But most of the population would have owned very little in the way of furniture. Examples of more elaborate furniture existed, such as the draw table, court cupboard, buffet and four-poster bed. But such items would have been found only in the very grandest of houses.

Another item of furniture that should be mentioned here is the Bible box. Most families that could afford furniture would surely have owned a Bible, and it would have been a valued possession. Something to keep the Bible in was needed. Bible boxes were often just miniature chests, but sometimes they were made with a stand to rest them on and had a sloping top on which the Bible could be placed for reading.

Furniture of the seventeenth century differed very little from that of the sixteenth. However, certain notable developments did take place. Chairs began to be upholstered, and there was seen to be a need for a smaller, more versatile type of table. The gate-leg table has been made in one form or another ever since its introduction then, and it has proved to be the most popular and versatile type of table ever made.

Possibly the most significant event at this time, at least as far as we are concerned, was the introduction of veneering. The introduction of veneering into English furniture-making meant that an entirely new form of carcase construction had to be used. If the entire surface of a piece of furniture was to be covered in veneer, it was obvious that panelled construction, especially with pegged joints, would be no good at all. A new method of building up a carcase with flat surfaces had to be adopted. This new method of construction was to continue throughout the eighteenth and nineteenth centuries, even at those times when veneering was out of favour.

During this period there appeared a great number of entirely new pieces of furniture, brought about by a change in the life-style and an increase in prosperity. Books, which had hitherto been kept in chests, now had cabinets of their own, often with glazed doors. Cabinets for writing, longcase clocks, games tables, china cabinets and mirrors all appeared at this time.

The introduction of mahogany around 1720 greatly affected the construction and indeed the design of English furniture in the eighteenth century. This early type of mahogany came from central and northern South America and was dark in colour, with a rather plain grain. After about 1750 Cuban mahogany began to be used, sometimes with curl and fiddle-back grain, the finest examples of which were kept for veneer. In the second half of the eighteenth century the lighter-coloured

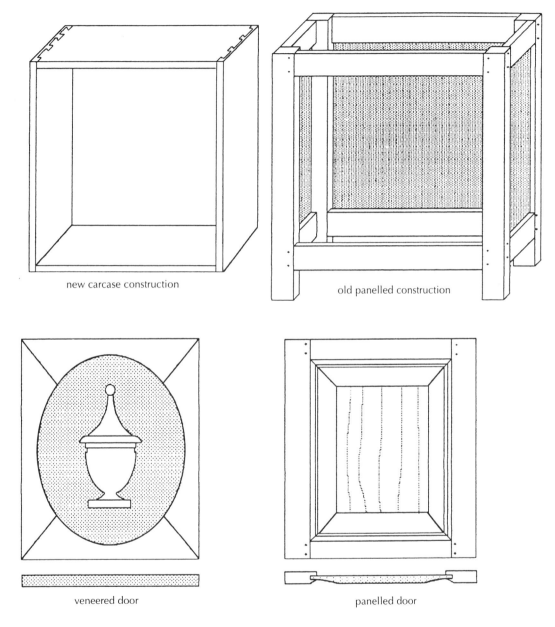

new carcase construction

old panelled construction

veneered door

panelled door

Fig. 1   Methods of carcase and door construction.

Honduras mahogany was the principal timber used.

Although I have said that the new form of construction introduced for veneering purposes remained in use throughout the eighteenth century, there was a return to the panelled construction of earlier times in the case of cabinet doors. Although mahogany was a very attractive timber as far as colour was concerned, it was regarded as having a rather plain grain. This was compensated for by a return to panelled doors and carving as a means of decoration. Chairs, on the other hand, which were largely made in the solid anyway, were little affected by the introduction of the new timber.

THE CHEST

Early chests were very crude affairs, consisting of planks of wood nailed together and with a top that lifted by means of a pivot or pin hinge at the back, the strap hinge not putting in an appearance until the end of the thirteenth century. Their basic construction remained much the same until the end of the fifteenth century, when framed-up panelling began to appear with mortise and tenon joints. Many changes in style occurred due to the influence of the Renaissance, but we are really interested here in the construction of furniture. In the seventeenth century the chest began to change. Two drawers were added at the bottom of the chest, so that items stored at the bottom could be reached without rummaging through the entire contents. This new item of furniture became known as the mule chest. Drawers proved to be such a good idea that eventually, towards the end of the seventeenth century, chests were made with nothing but drawers, and the chest of drawers, proper, was born. Later seventeenth-century chests with drawers can be found, both freestanding on bun or bracket feet and also on separate stands with turned supports.

Walnut began to be used in England in the last quarter of the seventeenth century, when much of the furniture was veneered and covered in the most elaborate marquetry. The drawers of this period, however, were quite crudely constructed, with thick sides, often nailed onto the back

A carved oak English chest circa 1690.

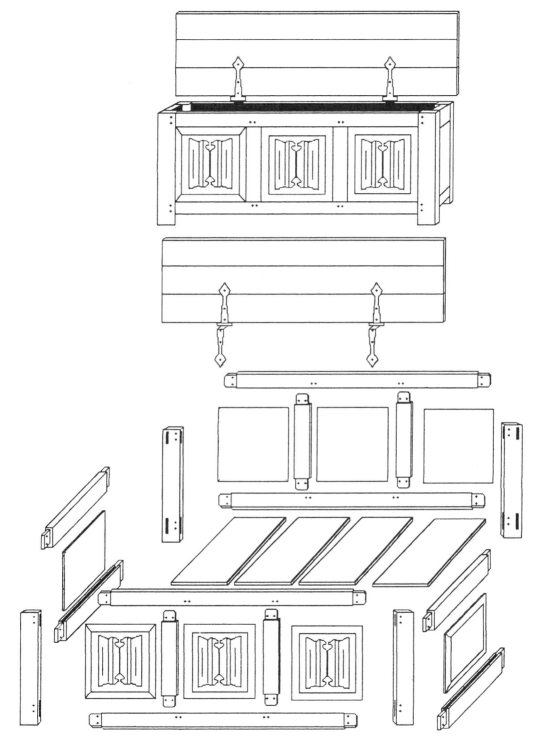

Fig. 2   Construction of a medieval framed chest.

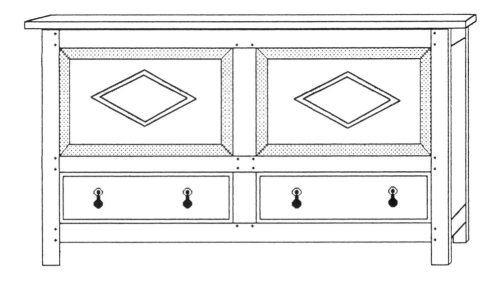

Fig. 3   A mule chest.

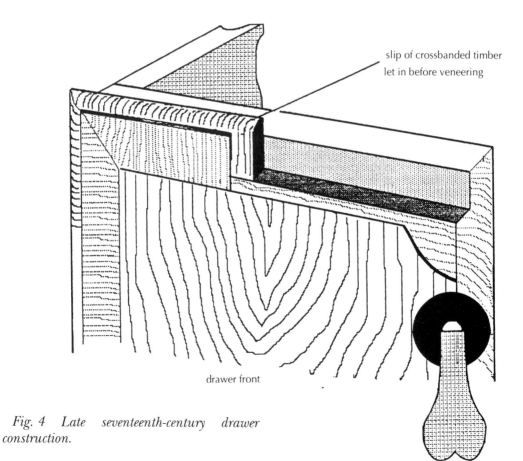

slip of crossbanded timber
let in before veneering

drawer front

Fig. 4   Late   seventeenth-century   drawer construction.

and into a rebate in the drawer front. Grooves cut in the sides of the drawer fitted over runners on the inside of the chest carcase, so that the drawer was suspended inside the chest. The drawer front at this time had a lip around the edge that prevented dust from entering the drawer and which acted as a drawer stop. With the walnut-veneered drawer front, this meant that a slip of cross-banded solid timber had to be let into the edge of the drawer before it was veneered.

The eighteenth century saw several changes in drawer construction. Drawer linings, of oak or pine, became progressively finer, and drawer runners were placed on the bottoms of the drawer sides to run on bearers along the inside of the chest carcase. The edge of drawer fronts were finished off with a quarter-round bead, or later with cock-beading. The dovetail joints of drawers also became progressively finer as the century progressed. The grain of the bottom boards ran from front to back until about 1780,

A Georgian mahogany chest-on-chest or tallboy.

when they begin to be seen running from side to side. A separate dust strip with a quarter-round top and rebate to accept the drawer bottom came into use around 1830.

THE CHAIR

In the early days of furniture development the chair was more than just a piece of furniture; it was also a symbol of status and authority. Most households would have been lucky to have had proper stools, let alone a chair. Even important homes might have had no more than one chair, and that would have been a large and

Fig. 5 Seventeenth-century chest with separate stand.

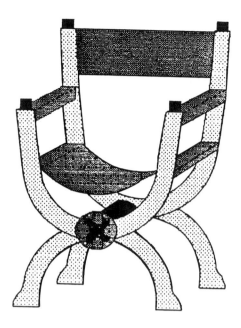

Fig. 6 X-frame chair, originally covered in velvet secured with gilt nails and capped with metal finials, c. 1550.

imposing piece of furniture. Chairs of the sixteenth century were either of X-frame construction, or they had a seat resembling an oak coffer with a straight back and arms. The construction of these chairs was virtually the same as that of chests, with panelled sides and backs, and mortise and tenon joints held in place with pegs. The chair gradually evolved from this into the chair we know today, the upright stiles of the chest-like construction becoming legs as the panels themselves were left out, and the bottom cross-stiles becoming understretchers.

The next development in chair construction came after the Restoration in 1660, when the backs of chairs were often left open rather than panelled, the top rail being arcaded and joined to a rail just above seat level by turnings. Many of these chairs would be made without arms, to accommodate the large dresses of the time, like the farthingale chair of this time. Chairs in general were becoming more

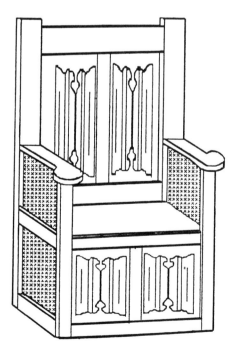

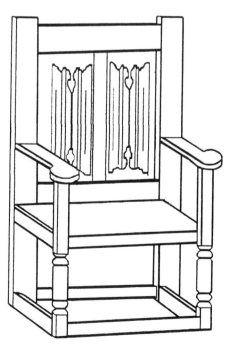

Fig. 7 Development of panelled chair design.

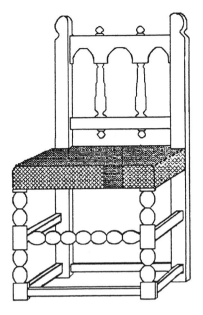

Fig. 8   Farthingale chair.

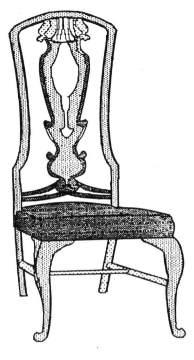

Fig. 9   A Queen Anne chair with shaped splat and cabriole legs.

delicate, and bobbin and barley-twist turnings were much in evidence.

Towards the close of the seventeenth century, chair backs became much taller, and arms had by this time acquired a definite downward slope. Many chairs at this time had seats consisting of a frame with canework, onto which would be placed a cushion. These seat frames, instead of being mortise and tenoned, were housed into the uprights of the back. The top of the front legs ended in a round dowel or peg onto which the seat frame fitted.

After the turn of the century a new type of chair was introduced from Holland. This new chair had a shaped splat, often in the form of a stylized urn, jointed between the head and seat rails. It is this style of chair that people refer to today as being Queen Anne style. Note the other very important feature that puts in an appearance at about this time, the cabriole leg.

Although styles changed considerably over the next two centuries, the basic construction of the chair remained fundamentally the same, except for the gradual disappearance of the understretchers.

THE TABLE

Tables of the fifteenth and sixteenth centuries would mostly have been of trestle construction for dining purposes, and would in many cases have been removed once dining was over. There were two types of trestle table. One had free-standing trestles at intervals along its length, the other had large, shaped supports at each end which were united by rails or stretchers that passed through them and were secured by wedges. When these wedges were removed the whole table could be taken apart with ease. Joined tables were also in use at this time but, generally speaking, tables were not specialized and

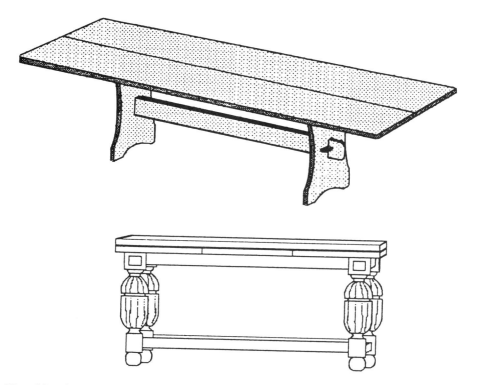

Fig. 10   A simple trestle table (top); a draw-table (bottom).

any table would be used for a multitude of purposes. The first extending tables put in an appearance around 1600. These tables were of the joined type and had a pull-or draw-out section at each end.

The mid-seventeenth century saw the arrival of the gate-leg table and a decline in the practice of dining in the great hall. Many homes began to have a separate room set aside for dining, and the gate-leg was the most widely used type of table.

With the introduction of mahogany around 1720, dining tables were made with cabriole legs, one of which would swing out on either side to support the flaps. A new type of dining table came into use around 1750. This consisted of a centre table with two square-section flaps supported on gate-legs and two half-round or D-end sections which could be used as side-tables when not required for dining.

The next advance in dining-table construction appears in the first quarter of the nineteenth century, when the two ends of the table were connected by a concertina or lazy-tongs action which enabled them to be pulled apart and additional leaves fitted. The table, however, that is most commonly associated with the early nineteenth century is the pillar dining table. These tables consist of a top supported on a pillar with three or four splay legs, and they were made with any number of pillars.

Probably the best method of extending a table was devised by the Victorians: a table with a turned leg at each corner, for good support with no tipping, and two separate tops connected by a system of rails that slid against one another. These tops slid apart, or wound open, by means of a large metal screw assembly, for the leaves to be inserted.

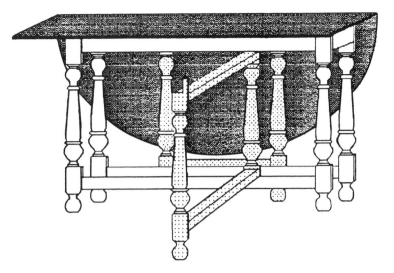

*Fig. 11   Gate-leg table with one leaf removed to
show underframe.*

Late seventeenth-century style gate-leg table.

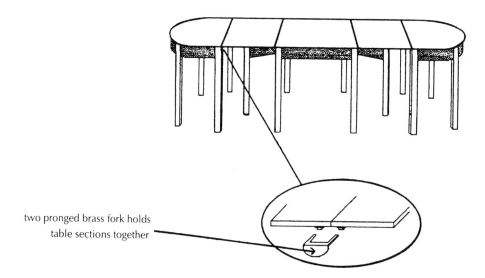

two pronged brass fork holds
table sections together

Fig. 12   Three-section dining table comprising a centre section with two drop-leaves and two end sections for use as side-tables when not required for dining.

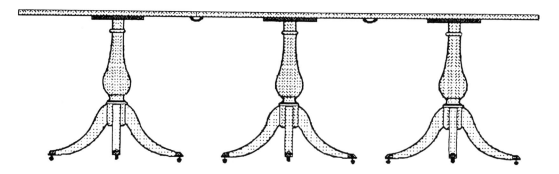

Fig. 13   Early nineteenth-century pillar table.

THE SIDEBOARD

It was not until the early years of the eighteenth century that a side-table, usually with a marble top, began to appear in dining rooms. These tables had no drawers or cupboards, and resembled the console and pier-tables of the time. Later on these tables were made with free-standing pedestals at each side, on which would stand a container for cutlery or an urn for water. Sometimes a wine cooler or cellaret would accompany the table and be stored underneath. Towards the end of the century the table and its side pedestals were joined together to form a single piece of furniture, and the sideboard as we understand it today was born. The use of a separate wine container was discontinued and a cellaret drawer included in one of the pedestals.

Fig. 14   Development of the sideboard.

two

Glossary of Furniture Types and Wood

SOME TYPES OF FURNITURE

It is not my intention to include a fully comprehensive listing here, as most types of furniture and their uses will be well known, or at least obvious from the name – everyone knows what a card-table or chair is. Here I want only to clarify things if there is possible confusion as to which term to use, or if there is a name that is not commonly used today, but which you may come up against at auction or in your local antique shop.

Buffet These days usually thought of as the large, open oak shelves of the late sixteenth and early seventeenth centuries, similar to the court cupboard. Both Georgian and Victorian examples can also be found, but these usually have one tier above a cupboard base.

Two-drawer Georgian mahogany buffet.

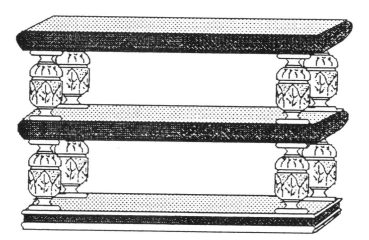

Fig. 15   A buffet.

A Georgian mahogany bureau with cock-beaded drawers and bracket feet.

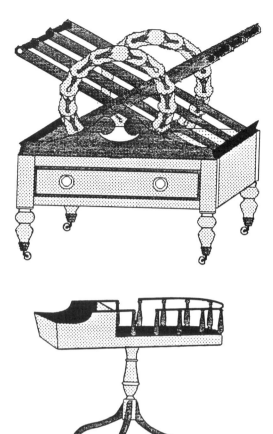

Fig. 16   A music canterbury (top) and a plate canterbury (bottom).

An inlaid display cabinet with concave glazed sides.

Bureau   This usually refers to a desk with drawers or cupboards below a sloping fall front, which is supported when open for writing.

Cabinet   Can refer to any piece of furniture with doors or small drawers in which to keep or display articles of value.

Canterbury   This term can be applied to a piece of furniture for holding sheet music, or one for holding plates, knives and forks.

Cellaret   Receptacle for wine bottles,

GLOSSARY OF FURNITURE TYPES AND WOOD

An unusual two-drawer mahogany music canterbury.

usually kept under a sideboard or side-table.

Chaise-longue A day-bed or couch with upholstered back.

Chest Container for household goods or clothes with a lift-up lid. A chest with two drawers in the base would be called a mule chest.

Chest of drawers As the name implies, a chest with the interior completely taken up with drawers.

Chest-on-chest Literally one chest of drawers on top of another; also known as a tallboy (see page 17).

Chiffonier Usually a cupboard with one or two doors, surmounted by one or more shelves (see page 27).

Coaster A device taking many different

A good-quality Victorian chaise-longue.

A William IVth mahogany chiffonier.

forms, used for circulating food and drink around the table.

Commode   This term can apply to a very decorative cabinet or chest of drawers intended for the drawing-room primarily as a decorative piece, or to any small cabinet containing a chamber-pot.

Couch   It is difficult to make a distinction between couch, day-bed or sofa, as any of these terms may be used to describe a piece of furniture used for reclining or taking repose in the daytime.

Credenza   A drawing-room cabinet with a large central door and two corner-end cabinets, usually with convex glass doors. The central door often has a porcelain plaque in the centre.

Cupboard   Originally a cupboard was literally a board or shelf on which to

A Victorian walnut and marquetry credenza.

A Victorian burr-walnut davenport with brass gallery.

place items. A cupboard enclosed by doors would have been known as an aumbry. However, these days the term refers to a cabinet with doors made of wood. Any piece of furniture with glass doors would more properly be referred to as a cabinet.

Davenport A small writing desk with a sloping top and drawers down one side. Early examples had a top that could be slid forward for writing. Later examples have a fixed top, overhanging at the front to accommodate the legs of the user.

Desk A table-like piece of furniture for reading or writing on, having a sloping top. Later the sloping top was placed on top of a chest of drawers, and this became the 'bureau'. Another type of desk, known as a pedestal desk, was later developed

with a flat top supported on two pedestals, each being fitted with drawers. The top section, which was itself fitted with drawers, often had a leather insert on the writing surface. Sometimes these desks were made with drawers on both sides and were known as 'partners' desks'.

Dresser This usually refers to a piece of furniture intended for use in the kitchen or parlour, with drawers and/or cupboards below a superstructure of shelves.

Dumb-waiter Tiers or trays fixed to a central column with a tripod base. They were generally placed diagonally at the corners of the dining table for the diners to help themselves.

Library steps As the name implies, these steps were used in order to obtain books from high shelves. They did not really put in an appearance until about the mid-eighteenth century, when larger bookcases meant that higher shelves could not simply be reached by standing

Fig. 17 A food hutch.

on a stool or chair. They fall into two distinct types: those that actually look like steps, and those that pretend to be something else. The latter type, sometimes referred to as metamorphic furniture, is most often found disguised as a chair, with the seat hinged so that the back can be tipped over the front to form the steps. However there are examples of tables and other cabinets concealing or turning into library steps.

Ottoman   A long, low, upholstered seat.

Sconce   A candle-holder or lantern attached to a wall or other upright surface such as the front of an upright piano.

Screen   Screens fall into three categories. There are large folding screens used to screen off draughts. There are smaller screens, sometimes on poles and sometimes sliding up and down between uprights, used to screen off the heat of the fire. Lastly there are small pole screens, used to screen a candle from draughts.

Settee and sofa   These two are closely related and are basically seats with back and arms for more than one person. The only real distinction is that a sofa allows for reclining.

Settle   These days we think of the settle as a wooden seat with a high back and arm, often with a chest in the seat.

Regency caned settee with painted decoration.

An unusual curved settle.

A mahogany bow-front sideboard raised on tapered supports with spade feet.

Sideboard Item of furniture used in the dining room for holding plates, wine and accessories, and developed for this purpose from the side-table.

Squab Name given to any upholstered removable seat or cushion.

Table, console A table intended to stand against a wall. Console tables are of bracket construction – that is to say, they are attached to the wall, and have no legs at the back, the front being supported often on elaborate scrolls and carvings.

Table, dressing A piece of furniture for holding brushes and other toilet requisites, often with a knee-hole for sitting at. They would often have either a separate dressing or toilet mirror, or have such a mirror or mirrors attached to uprights as part of the piece itself. They are found in all

shapes and sizes, but anything fitted with washing facilities would fall into the category of washstand rather than dressing table.

Table, gate-leg A table having flaps supported on a leg which swings out and has stretchers top and bottom forming a gate (see page 21). Any table supported in this manner where the leg does not have a bottom stretcher should be referred to as a drop-leaf table.

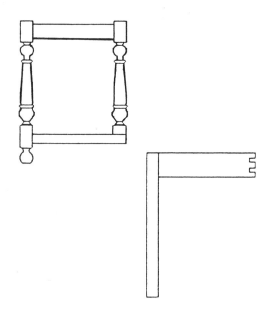

Fig. 18   Gate-leg for gate-leg table.
Fly-leg for drop-leaf table.

Table, library and writing Normally any small table that has a leather top or which was obviously intended for writing at would be referred to as a writing table. Larger or more elaborate versions can be referred to as library tables. Sometimes the distinction between library table and desk can be quite obscure, but a library table is perhaps more likely to be fitted with cupboards rather than just drawers, and would possibly be large enough for more than one person at a time to use.

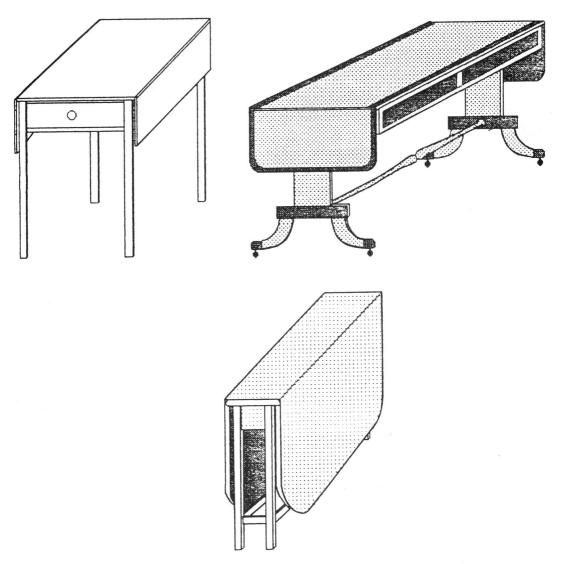

Fig. 19   Pembroke table; sofa table; Sutherland table.

Table, Pembroke   A small occasional table, possibly used originally as a breakfast table, having flaps supported by a hinged bracket on the long side of the top. The name is thought to come from the first person to order such a table, the Countess of Pembroke.

Table, pier   So called because they were intended to stand against that part of the wall between the windows of a room. These tables would often have a tall narrow mirror, or pier-glass, above them which helped to add light to the room.

Table, sofa   A table intended to be used behind or in front of a sofa, having flaps

*A mahogany Pembroke table on turned
and fluted supports.*

A Regency maghogany sofa table.

supported by a hinged bracket on the ends, or short side, of the top.

Table, Sutherland A flap table ranging in size from small occasional right up to dining. The flaps are supported on a swing-out leg on the long side of the top. The Sutherland table has a very narrow top with the leaves down; however, the leaves themselves are large in comparison and when let down reach almost to the floor.

A bow-front corner washstand circa 1780.

A Victorian Sutherland table with splayed bottom turned legs.

Torchère A stand for a candle or lamp.

Wash-stand At first a cabinet with doors and/or a drawer in which would be a receptacle for jug and basin and other toilet requirements. Later on, wash-stands were made as part of a bedroom suite. They would be made to match the dressing table to a large extent, but with a marble top on which a jug and basin could be placed.

What-not Portable stand or tiers of shelves intended for display.

SOME TYPES OF WOOD

Amboyna A light-brown timber from the West Indies, with a rich colour and a bird's-eye figure to the grain. Amboyna was used in the eighteenth century both for decorative bandings and occasionally to cover whole surfaces.

Ash A very pale, almost whitish wood with pale brown veining. Sometimes mistaken for imported white oak. Ash is mostly to be found in country furniture, such as Windsor chairs.

GLOSSARY OF FURNITURE TYPES AND WOOD

Beech A light-brown timber with specks in the grain. Beech takes stain very well and was the main choice of timber for furniture that was to be grained so as to resemble another wood, such as rosewood. Beech is extensively used for upholstered furniture and seat frames because it grips nails and tacks. If you hammer a tack into a piece of beech and then remove it, you will observe that the hole left by the tack will have a tendency to close up slightly, showing how it 'grips'.

Birch Sometimes used instead of beech for cheap furniture as it also takes stain very well; in the nineteenth century used as a substitute for satinwood.

Boxwood Hard, yellow-coloured wood used as an inlay from as early as the sixteenth century.

Cedar A light reddish-brown wood, used for boxes and drawer linings. Cedar has a strong but pleasant aroma.

Coromandel A broad-streaked timber of the ebony family, light brown with very dark streaks, used both as a veneer and for decorative bandings in the late eighteenth and early nineteenth centuries.

Ebony A very heavy wood, almost black in colour and used mostly for small turnings and decorative work.

Elm A hard, brown timber with irregular grain, found mostly in country furniture.

Fruitwood Apple and pear are a light reddish-brown with a close grain. Both were stained black and used as a substitute for ebony. Cherry is more red in colour and was used for some country furniture. Old cherry can at first glance be mistaken for mahogany.

Kingwood Sometimes known as 'princes wood', similar to rosewood but much lighter in colour.

Laburnum Yellow with brown markings, often sliced across the end of the log and used as oyster-shell veneer.

Lime Whitish in appearance with very little grain, this timber was much favoured by carvers.

Mahogany Principal furniture wood from the early eighteenth century. It has many different varieties and ranges in colour from dark red to light brown. Mahogany is used both in the solid and as a veneer. The first type of mahogany used for furniture in England was imported from San Domingo in the West Indies and was known as Spanish mahogany; this had a straight grain and was very dark in colour. Later, Cuban mahogany was favoured, as it was found to produce fine figured grain. Towards the end of the century, Honduras mahogany was largely used; this was lighter in weight and colour and had a more open grain.

Maple Very white in colour and used in veneer. The bird's-eye maple used as a veneer in the nineteenth century is cut from the American sugar maple.

Oak English oak is hard and heavy and varies in colour from light to dark brown. Early oak was riven, that is to say it was split down the length, in line with the medullary rays. The trunk was first cut into quarters, and then these quarters were split into more suitable sizes. All the planks split in this way would be wedge-shaped in section and would all display the distinctive patches of the medullary rays across the grain. Later, when oak was sawn rather than riven, the boards were quarter-sawn. Sawing was done to reduce the amount of waste, but only those boards that most closely followed the line of the medullary rays would show the silver patches. These days most oak is plain sawn across the trunk, and only the boards from the middle of the trunk will have the marks of the medullary rays. I have heard it said that all early oak was quarter-sawn, but this is not strictly true, as it was observed that wood that did not show the medullary rays was far better for veneering on, and some boards must have been produced for this purpose.

Pine   Soft white timber, used for carcase construction and drawer linings.

Rosewood   Varieties of rosewood come from both South America and India. Rich brown in colour with dark streaks. Very hard and heavy, used mostly as a veneer in the Regency and Victorian periods; however, some examples of its use in the solid can be found, although these will in the main be chairs that are not practical to veneer. Rosewood has always been a desirable and expensive timber; many items were produced in an inferior wood and simulated to look like rosewood.

Satinwood   A rich yellow colour with good figure or straight grain, used mostly as a veneer in the late eighteenth century. Regained popularity in the later Victorian period, although birch and chestnut were often used as a substitute.

Tulipwood   Yellowish brown with red and purple stripes, used mostly for cross-bandings.

Walnut   English and European walnut is light to dark brown in colour, with a rich streaked grain. Some trees have a malformation on the trunk from which burr walnut veneer is cut, with its very intricate curling grain. Another type of walnut also in use was American black walnut, or Virginia walnut. This walnut was used in great part for dining tables in the early eighteenth century and can look very similar to faded mahogany.

Yew   Distinctive streaked reddish-brown grain that fades to a more uniform nut brown. Used for some country furniture and Windsor chairs.

three

The basics of furniture restoration

THE WORKSHOP

If you are going to undertake the restoration of antique furniture on a more or less regular basis, you will need a workshop, or at the very least an area set aside for that purpose where items can be left overnight in cramps and the general mess caused by woodwork can be tolerated. You will need somewhere to store tools and materials. With modern cabinet-making you can buy what you need when you need it, but this is not the case with restoration. You will need to gradually build up a stock of old timber, salvaged from pieces of furniture that are too far gone to be saved. These pieces are getting harder to find, as more and more of them become worth restoring themselves and more and more restorers are seeking them out. Old timber is not the only thing you will have to start saving, however. In fact the restorer should throw almost nothing away. Even the smallest offcut of timber or veneer might have just the pattern of grain you need for a particular job, one day. Old handles, keys, hand-cut screws and nails, blown glass, bits of moulding or decoration – the list is endless – all must be saved and stored in such a way that they can be easily found when required. There is little that is more frustrating for the restorer than searching fruitlessly for an item that you know you have, but can't find.

So your work area must have room to work, it must have room to store timber and other useful items, it must have good natural light for colouring and polishing, it must have a power supply and above all, if you intend to strip off old polish with paint remover, it must be well ventilated. Paint strippers are dangerous if heated or used near a flame. In normal use the fumes are harmful, and a proper chemical mask is strongly recommended. The fumes are heavier than air, so any extractor fan should be fitted at ground level.

THE BENCH

In my own workshop, I have found it useful to have a good firm bench, with as large a woodworking vice as possible, a large table on which I can stand chairs and other items whilst they are being worked on or cramped up, and a low platform or cut-down table for standing larger items on in order to bring them up to a good working height. This is especially useful when, for instance, you need to work on the front of a chest of drawers: the chest can be turned on its back and still be at a comfortable height.

Working height is a very important thing to consider when setting up a workshop. Benches tend to come like tables, at a standard height; but people don't. Try out a few things on your bench, like planing a piece of wood, both in the vice and on the bench top. Is it at a comfortable height, or do you find you have to stoop? Back problems have been the curse of many a bench worker, and I wonder how many of these problems could have been avoided by simply adding some height to the bench. Always remember to hold your work secure and at a comfortable height; many times I

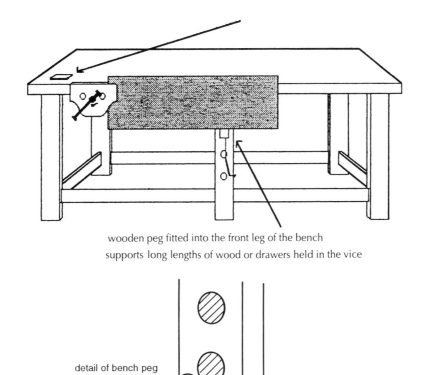

wooden peg fitted into the front leg of the bench
supports long lengths of wood or drawers held in the vice

detail of bench peg

Fig. 20   Bench.

have seen someone attempting to take apart a chair, holding steadfastly onto one leg or rail, whilst hammering at another; all this strenuous work being carried out, stooping over the chair on the floor. How much better for both chair and back, if held firmly in the vice.

The bench must have a good solid top and legs, to withstand hammering, a large, good-quality vice and a bench stop against which wood can be placed for planing. I have also found it useful to have large holes drilled in the front of the centre leg, into which I can put a wooden support for items such as drawers that can only be partially held in the vice.

ACCESSORIES

Shooting board

The shooting board is designed to allow you to plane smaller pieces of wood across the grain; however, once you have got used to using one, you will no doubt find a multitude of uses for it. One such use is for making those little adjustments to mitres or the ends of a new piece of cock-beading.

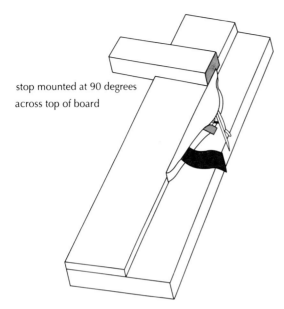

stop mounted at 90 degrees
across top of board

Fig. 21   A 90-degree shooting board.

It is a good idea to have at least two shooting boards: one of 90 degrees and one of 45 degrees.

Bench hook

The bench hook is a very simple device on which you can easily hold a small piece of wood that needs to be cut across the grain.

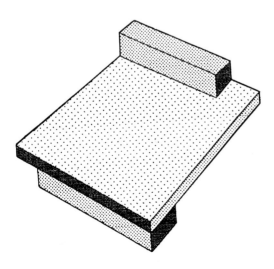

Fig. 22   A bench hook.

It consists of a flat piece of timber with a batten on the top front edge, against which the piece of wood to be cut can be held, and a similar batten on the bottom back edge that catches against the front of the bench.

Mitre block

The mitre block, or mitre box, is another simple device, used as the name implies for cutting mitres. If a mitre block is to be of any use, of course, it must be accurate and well made. Various types of mitre block are available, including some that have cramps to hold the wood whilst it is being cut. These days it is possible to buy large mitre-cutting sets which will cut even large cornices very accurately.

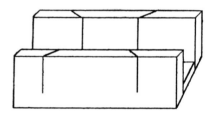

Fig. 23   A mitre block.

Bureau support

Sometimes cabinets will have to be turned upside down, to enable you to work on the feet or bottom. Chests should be no problem, but a bureau needs to be supported or it will topple over. A simple method of overcoming this is to have a batten with an adjustable height cross-member that can be secured under one of the bureau stiles to prevent it toppling forward.

Fret-saw cutting block

For use with a hand-held fret-saw; it is basically a flat piece of wood with a V-shape cut in it and some form of leg or extension underneath, so that it can be held in a vice. The piece of wood to be cut

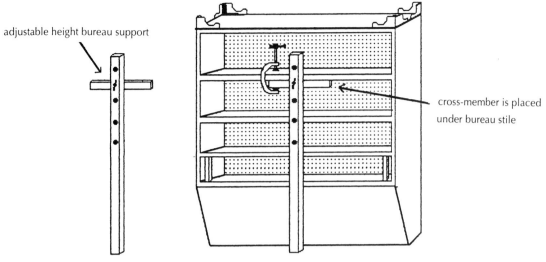

adjustable height bureau support

cross-member is placed under bureau stile

bureau support prevents bureau from toppling forward when turned upside down

Fig. 24   A bureau support.

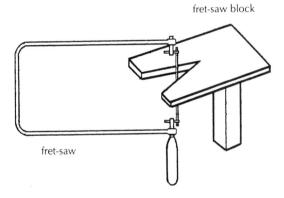

fret-saw block

fret-saw

Fig. 25   A fret-saw cutting block.

is held flat on the top surface and the fret-saw blade passes through the vee.

SOME USEFUL TOOLS

Cabinet scrape
The cabinet scrape is a tool that is seldom used by the amateur woodworker, but a very useful one to the restorer. The scrape is used to remove a very fine shaving of wood from table tops and the like before sanding. It is an ideal tool for cleaning up inlay and marquetry, and will remove plane marks from new surfaces and scratches and stains from old ones.

To sharpen a cabinet scrape you will need a fine file and a steel (a knife sharpener). First, file a straight edge on each long side of the scrape, and hone these edges on an oilstone so that you end up with four very sharp edges. The next step is to turn these edges over very slightly with the steel, creating a sharp burr on each side.

In use, the scrape is held with the fingers of each hand in front, curled around the sides and the thumbs pressed in the middle of the back of the tool, slightly bending it. The scrape is then pushed across the surface of the work, removing fine shaving.

Scratch-stock
The scratch-stock is a piece of steel that has been filed and shaped to make a moulding, or a groove for inlay. The shaped steel can be held in a piece of wood that acts as both handle and guide. When using the scratch-stock it is best to cut with a pushing action,

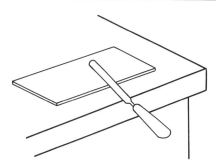

1. place scraper flat on its side and remove old burr with steel knife sharpener

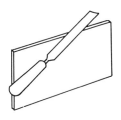

2. file to obtain straight edge

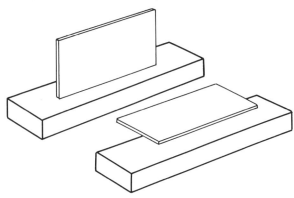

3. hone edges on oil stone to obtain four sharp edges

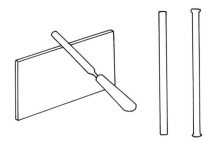

4. turn sharpened end over with steel

Fig. 26   Sharpening a cabinet scrape.

scratch stock

cutter

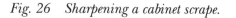

direction of cut

scratch stock

cut starts a little more this way each time

extra cutters

wooden block

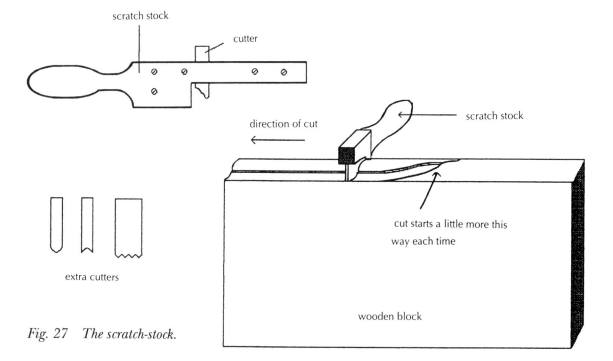

Fig. 27   The scratch-stock.

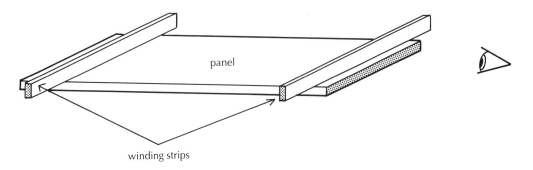

Fig. 28   Winding strips.

rather than drawing the blade towards you, and to start at the point farthest away, taking a small amount of wood only on each cut and slowly working back so that each new cut starts a little nearer to you. Starting at the farthest point means that you are always working with the grain, from a high point to a low one.

Winding Strips
Winding strips are two strips of straight timber, similar to those used to determine if the legs of a chair are uneven. They are used when planing a panel or other wide flat surface, to see if it is in wind. One winding strip is placed at either end of the panel, so that you can sight along the top and determine if the panel is in wind.

CHAPTER four

Dismantling furniture

SOME POINTS TO REMEMBER

Before it is possible to carry out any structural repairs to a piece of furniture, it is necessary to have a basic knowledge of how the piece in question was constructed – this concerns what type of joints were used, and which pieces were put together first. This knowledge is essential if the piece is to be dismantled without causing further damage.

Before I go into detail about specific pieces of furniture, there are one or two things which will be the same for most items. First, before attempting to take any joint apart, be sure that it will do so without putting a strain on any other joint, and make sure that it has not been nailed, pegged or screwed in any way. Sometimes nails are hard to spot – they can be quite small and they are not always put in from the outside of a leg, so examine carefully inside legs and seat frames. If a joint has been nailed, the offending nail will have to be removed before any attempt is made to move the joint. Damage will certainly result, otherwise. (The method employed in removing nails is explained on page 56.)

Always make sure that one part of the joint you are dismantling is held firmly in a vice – never be tempted to think that you or a colleague can hold it while it is knocked apart. A joint needs to be held firm when being knocked apart. A heavy hammer and block of wood should be used – a small hammer is much more likely to cause damage than a large one. A builder's lump hammer is by far the best for this purpose, but you will need a stout block of wood between the hammer and the job, to prevent marking. Never keep hammering at a joint; if it does not come apart easily, then another method of repair must be found.

Whenever a piece of furniture is to be dismantled, whether wholly or partly, it is always a good idea to clearly mark each joint, so that there is no chance of incorrect reassembly. In some cases this may seem completely unnecessary, but even then it can save time; there is little more infuriating than getting a chair half-assembled and then finding that a rail is upside-down or the wrong way around. Not only do tempers get frayed, but glue tends to start going off as well, so please mark all joints before dismantling. A little masking tape on each part of the joint can be marked with a pencil or felt-tip pen.

THE CHAIR

One piece of furniture above all others presents us with nearly all the problems we are ever likely to come across – the chair. It is the most difficult to make, the most difficult by far to repair successfully and it is the piece of furniture we use and abuse most often. It is expected to take the weight of even the heaviest of people, reaching, stretching and lounging, often imposing great strains on the smallest of joints. Small wonder, then, that chairs are the most frequent of visitors to the restoration workshop. Some repairs, of course, can be carried out without the necessity for dismantling, but more often than not at least some of the joints will have to come apart.

First, let us take a look at the most important differences in chair construction. Leaving upholstered furniture on one side for the moment, there are three main types. There is the Windsor chair, which can have all four legs and their stretchers removed without touching any of the back. There is the side-assembled chair, which has the sides glued together as two units and then has these units joined by the front seat rail and the various back members. Lastly there is the chair which has the back glued together as a unit, the front legs and front seat rail as another unit and then these two units joined by the side seat rails and any understretchers.

Headrails can also be of three distinct types. Some are mortise and tenoned between the uprights of the back, some are mortise and tenoned or dowelled onto the uprights and some are attached by means of a sliding dovetail joint. The last two of these have to be removed before the rest of the back can be dismantled. It is very important to take the chair apart in the

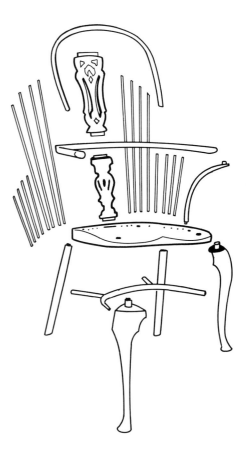

Fig. 29   The Windsor chair.

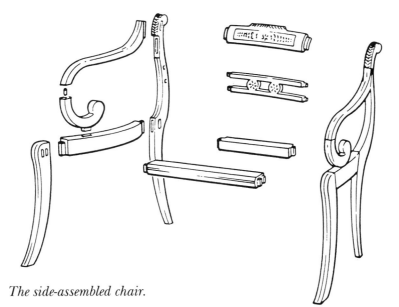

Fig. 30   The side-assembled chair.

43

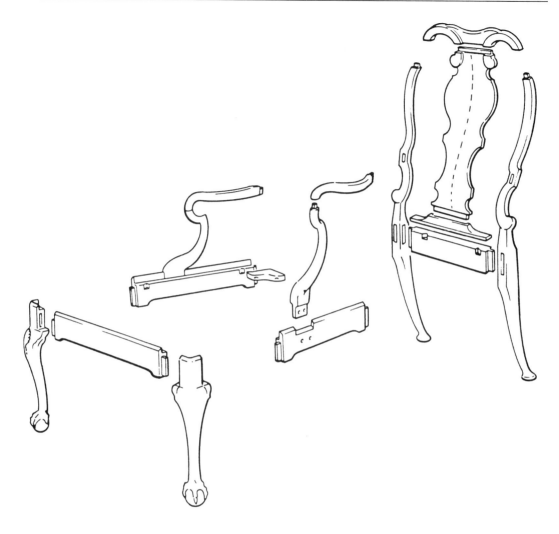

Fig. 31   The back-assembled chair.

correct order: because of the wedge shape of the seat, trying to remove the legs first from the side-constructed chair could well result in damage. The converse is true in the case of the back-assembled chair: here the front legs should be removed as a unit along with the front seat rail before being separated from each other.

Having determined exactly which joints need to come apart and in which order, the next task is to make sure that the joints have not been nailed or pegged in any way so as to prevent their safe separation. If joints have been nailed then the nails have

to be removed before proceeding further. The methods of removing nails and pegs are described later.

With the back-assembled chair, the front legs and back can be separated by turning the chair upside down and placing one siderail in the vice. In this position one front leg and one back leg can each be hammered apart, using a piece of soft wood between hammer and chair to prevent bruising the leg. This technique of using a buffer of soft wood should always be employed. It can be seen that a small amount of counter-pressure is required at

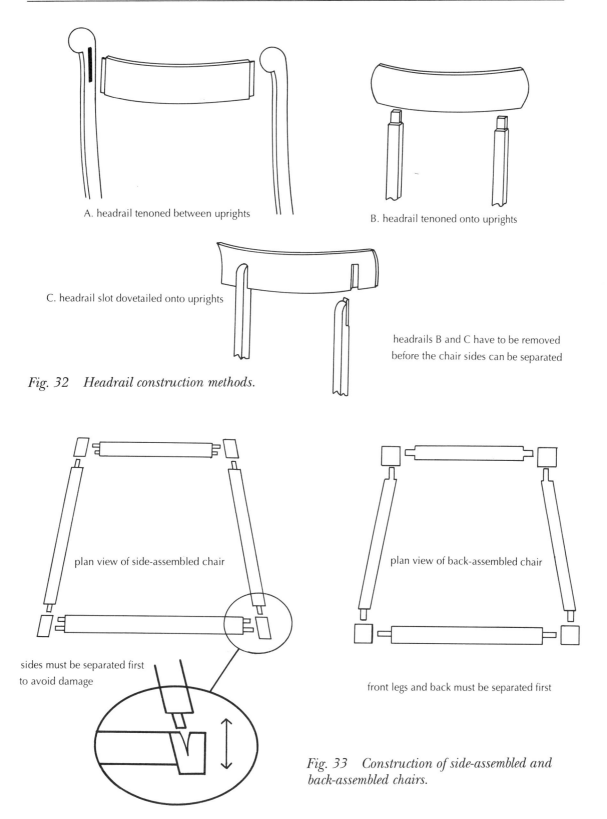

A. headrail tenoned between uprights

B. headrail tenoned onto uprights

C. headrail slot dovetailed onto uprights

headrails B and C have to be removed
before the chair sides can be separated

Fig. 32   Headrail construction methods.

plan view of side-assembled chair

plan view of back-assembled chair

sides must be separated first
to avoid damage

front legs and back must be separated first

*Fig. 33   Construction of side-assembled and
back-assembled chairs.*

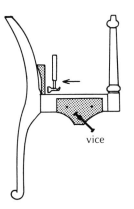

counter-pressure here → to ensure upright comes off squarely

vice

vice

Fig. 34   Separating a back-assembled chair.

the end of the leg, so as to ensure that it comes off square. When the joint starts to come apart it should only be opened half an inch or so (1–2cm) and then do the same to the other side so as not to spring the seat too far out of square as it comes apart. If the chair is side-assembled it can be handled in much the same way, except that this time the front seat rail goes in the vice first and the front legs are knocked apart about an inch or so (2–3cm). The headrail on this type chair can be of either type and will have to be removed first if it is attached with sliding dovetails. This is done by holding one upright securely in a vice and hammering the headrail upwards.

Strike as near as possible to the joint itself, but if the headrail does not come away easily then any repairs will have to be carried out with it in place. If any joint, not just a headrail, does not come apart relatively easily then no good will come from persisting. In a case where some joints come and some don't, then the loose joints can be sprung apart just a little and glue injected. The method of accomplishing this is described later in the book.

A NOTE ON CHAIR ARMS

Arms also have to be treated differently on side-assembled chairs, as they form an integral part of the side and are usually taken apart only after the sides have been separated; however, it will often be unnecessary, as in my experience these particular joints often stay much firmer than the rest of the chair. The same cannot be said, however, of the back-assembled chair: on these the arms always seem to be loose and need to be removed before the seat rails can be separated from the back uprights.

The arms on back-assembled chairs are normally attached to the backs by means of a screw through the upright, which is covered with a wooden fillet. However, sometimes they are tenoned into the upright.

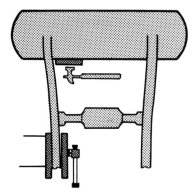

Fig. 35   Removing the headrail on a side-assembled chair.

This is likely to be the case if the arm attaches to the front rather than the side of the upright. They are normally attached to the arm support by tenon or dowel.

The arm supports on back-assembled chairs can be fitted either by being tenoned or dowelled onto the top of the seat rail. They can also be dowelled onto the top of the front leg, and they can be slot-dovetailed onto the seat rail or screwed onto the outside of the seat rail either from inside the rail or through the arm support itself. Great care must be taken, as it is not always obvious which method has been used. The fact that there are screws visible does not mean that there is no dovetail, and sometimes when the arm support is half-lapped over the seat rail there is also a tenon into the top of the rail.

The best course of action is to assume the arm is dovetailed. Remove any screws. Place the seat rail in a vice and tap the arm support upwards, as this is the way it will have to move whether it is tenoned or dovetailed.

CORNER BLOCKS

Many chairs are fitted with corner blocks to give them added strength. These blocks are of two distinct types. The first is found on upholstered seats and consists of a piece of wood let into the top of each seat rail either side of the leg and some three inches from it. The second type of block is shaped to fit between the seat rails and to be both glued and screwed to them. If this latter type of block is fitted accurately, and by that I mean that it should be a perfect fit against both seat rails, then it adds much greater strength to the chair. Even those chairs that have the greater strength supplied by understretchers will benefit from well-fitted corner blocks. I have emphasized that these blocks must be well fitted, and it is very possible that after a chair has been taken apart and reglued, and maybe even had some repair or other carried out, the original blocks will no longer fit so well. They must be adjusted before refitting. Ensure that when one side is held against

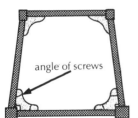

corner blocks glued and screwed to seat frame.
This type of block can be used for any seat frame

corner blocks let into seat frame
used only for upholstered seat

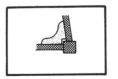

block fits well

block needs adjusting

screws at a slight angle to pull block
in tight to seat frame

Fig. 36   Corner blocks.

the seat rail without rocking, the other side fits just as well. Only then should the blocks be reglued and screwed. Note that the screws are put in at a slight angle so as to pull the block in tight.

DISMANTLING THE CABINET

BASIC NON-VENEERED CONSTRUCTION

The basic construction of most cabinets consists of top and bottom boards dovetailed along the ends onto the sides of the cabinet. This is true of most chests of drawers, bureaux, bureau bookcases, cupboards, kneehole desks and other cabinets of a basic square shape. Any crossrails or stiles are either tenoned, housed or slot-dovetailed into the sides; close inspection will be needed to determine which

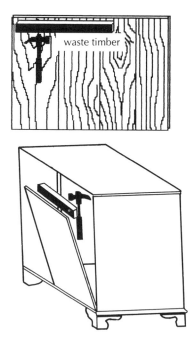

waste timber should span more than one plank

Fig. 37   Removing a nailed back.

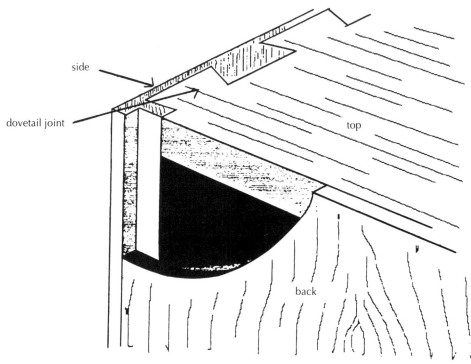

Fig. 38   Chest construction – detail.

method is used. The back is usually only nailed into a rebate at the rear, but sometimes, when the back is panelled, it may be found that it has been secured with screws. If the back has been screwed then removal is a simple matter of taking out the screws (see notes on removing old screws on page 56). However, if the back is nailed much more care is needed. The back will have to be hammered out from inside, which is accomplished by hammering along the top, bottom and sides of the back with a large hammer against a stout piece of timber which spans a good portion of the back across the grain. In the case of a panelled back which has been nailed, the danger of splitting along the grain when hammering is not so great, but the same technique should be employed. Once the back is removed the rest of the cabinet can usually be dismantled if the joints are loose but a thorough check should be made to make sure there are no mouldings or bandings across joints which will come to harm. If there are, these will of course need to be dealt with first. This is not usually as bad as it sounds, because if the joint is loose

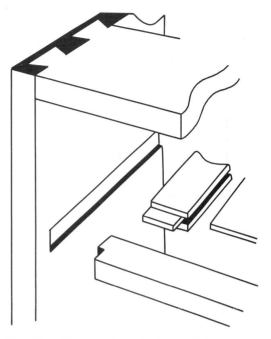

Fig. 39   Construction of stiles and drawer runners.

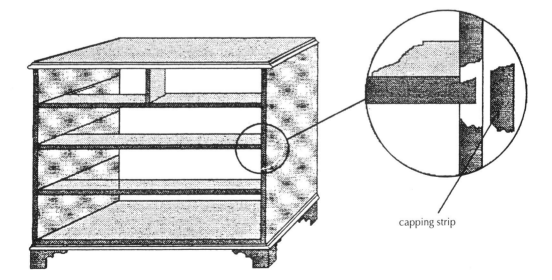

capping strip

Fig. 40   Capping strip – detail.

there will have been some movement and this will have broken any bond between the loose leg or stile and the moulding. Sometimes the moulding may have a pin in it as well as having been glued, but it should be possible to lift the moulding slightly with a fine blade or palette knife and insert a hacksaw blade under the moulding to cut the pin.

Top and bottom boards which are dovetailed onto the side should be hammered away in the same manner as removing the back, with a long piece of waste wood across the grain. Stiles are often slotted into rebates in the cabinet sides, as are drawer runners and dustboards, and then covered with a capping strip.

BASIC VENEERED CONSTRUCTION

The basic construction for veneered furniture is often as I have just described for non-veneered. The problem is that the joints can then be veneered over and all trace of a joint may be gone. This is especially true of articles such as veneered doors in which a door is constructed with conventional mortise and tenon joints, but would appear from the veneers to be mitred. If this is the case and there is no way of repairing the cabinet without taking it apart, it will be necessary to lift at least that portion of veneer covering the joint and then take the joint apart in the usual way.

DISMANTLING DRAWERS

Most of the drawers you will come across will be dovetailed front and back. Some very early or very crude ones may only be nailed, but in either case the sides will have to be hammered out sideways from the front and back, after the bottom has been removed. The bottoms of drawers are where any problems will lie. The easiest of

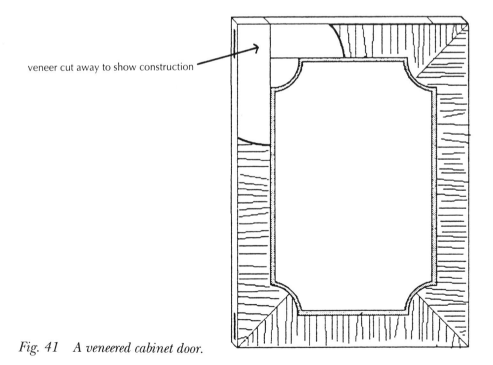

veneer cut away to show construction

Fig. 41 A veneered cabinet door.

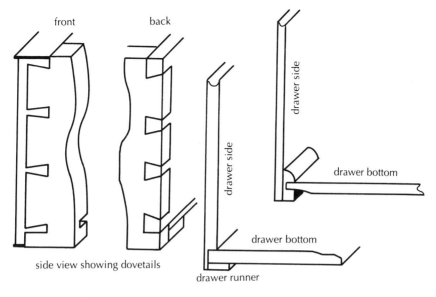

front   back

drawer side

drawer side

drawer bottom

drawer side

drawer bottom

side view showing dovetails

drawer runner

Fig. 42   Drawer construction.

drawers to dismantle is probably the better-quality Victorian drawer, as this will have the bottom sliding into a dust strip and secured with nails or screws into the underside of the back. All that has to be done to remove the bottom of these is to take out the screws, or, in the case of nails, prise the bottom and the back apart sufficiently to insert a hacksaw blade and cut the nails. The bottom can then be slid out with little effort.

Most other drawer bottoms are fitted into either a rebate or groove in the drawer side and the drawer runners glued onto both bottom and side, making it necessary to remove the runners before separating the sides. It may be possible to prise the drawer runner off if the glue is perished, otherwise it will be necessary to chop it away carefully with a hammer and chisel after first cutting with a tenon saw between the runner and the drawer side, in order to avoid damaging the drawer side.

With drawers, as with all other joints, use a block of wood between the job and the hammer. Choose a block which will span the whole depth of the drawer side

across the grain, as this will reduce the chance of splitting the side.

DISMANTLING TABLES

Tables come in all shapes and sizes – in fact the table is the piece of furniture which has the greatest variety of shapes, styles and uses. The basic table with four legs and a top will be mortise and tenoned together and the legs will be fitted in the same way as on a chair. To remove them, the apron, or side rail, should be held in a vice while the leg is hammered away using, as always, a soft block to protect the leg and using counter-pressure on the bottom of the leg to ensure that it comes off square.

Before this can be done it will no doubt be necessary to remove the top. Most tops are secured in one of two ways: either they are held on with screws or they are held with glue blocks. If they are held with screws then life is simple. The only problem that is likely to arise is if the screws are difficult to undo. (See notes on removing old screws, below.) If the top is

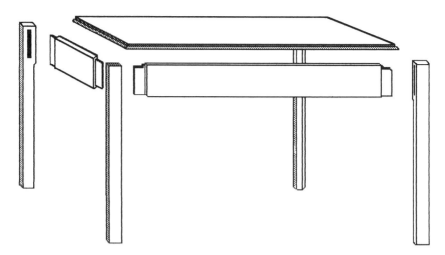

Fig. 43   Table construction.

held on with glue blocks then sometimes it is possible just to give the blocks a knock sideways with a hammer and this will dislodge them. If the first idea doesn't work then heat applied with an iron may do the trick. If not, then the block will have to be chiselled away a piece at a time and a new block made to replace it.

TABLES WITH DRAWERS

If a table is fitted with one or more drawers it is more than likely that the rail above the top drawer will be fitted to the leg by means of a dovetail joint, and this rail will have to be removed after the top has been taken off but before the mortise and tenon joints are separated.

TRIPOD TABLES

The legs on a tripod table may be attached either with dowels or by means of a slot dovetail. In the case of dowels the leg will have to be secured in a vice and the pillar hammered away from the leg. Be sure, as always, to place a wooden block between

the hammer and the pillar, to prevent damage. When the leg is attached by means of a slot dovetail, the pillar will have to be secured in the vice and the leg hammered downwards. The block used to prevent damage should be shaped to fit the leg. It is often the case that a metal plate has been screwed onto the underside of the legs and pillar and this will obviously have to be removed first (see notes on removing old screws).

To detach the top
Some tops, usually on the larger tables, are made to be detachable by means of thumb bolts on either side, which also act as a pivot for the tipping action of the table. However, many of the smaller tables are constructed so as to be one unit and in this case one of the two cross-stretchers under the top will have to be removed, to free the pillar from the top. The cross-stretchers are normally just screwed to the underside of the top, so not too much difficulty should be encountered. A good tip to remember when you have removed screws which are going to be replaced is to fill the screw holes with some soft wood such as poplar. If this is not done it may well be found on

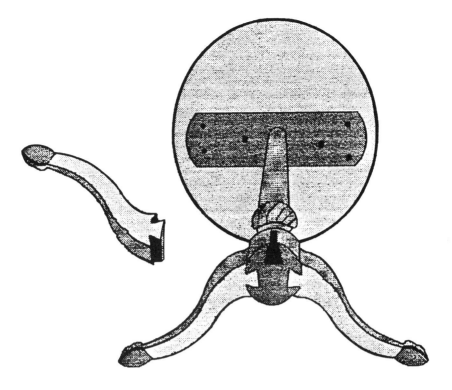

Fig. 44   Tripod table with slot dovetails.

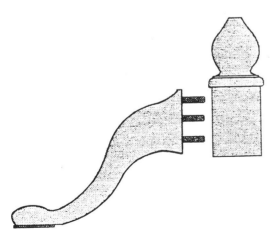

Fig. 45   Tripod table with dowel joints.

trying to replace the screws that they no longer do up tight.

Large tables of this type sometimes have an apron piece around the underside of the top, just in from the edge. These aprons are secured with screws which are covered with wooden plugs. (See notes on removing wooden plugs, below.) Small tripod tables which do not have a tip-up action usually have the top of the pillar mortised and tenoned into a cross-member which is then screwed onto the underside of the table top. The cross-member will be fitted across the grain of the top to help to prevent warping, and care must be taken in removing it as it is sometimes glued. If the cross-member is damaged or has wood-worm and needs to be replaced, it will be found that the tenons are wedged, and these will have to be drilled out before the joint can be separated.

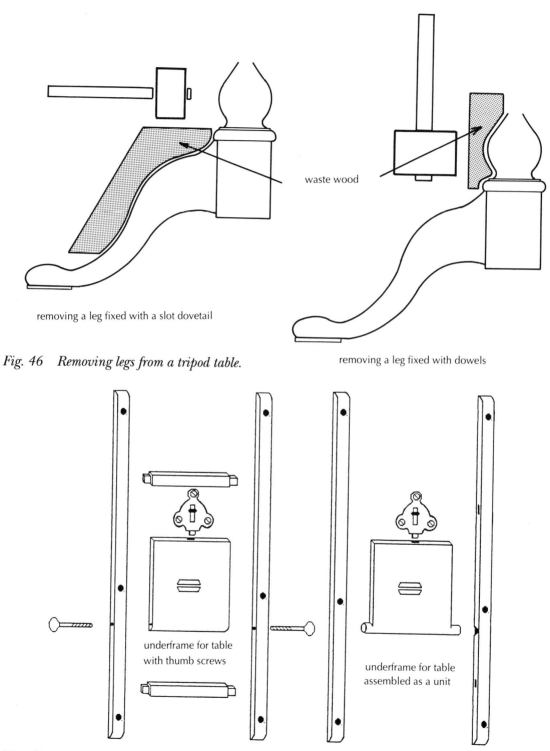

waste wood

removing a leg fixed with a slot dovetail

removing a leg fixed with dowels

Fig. 46   Removing legs from a tripod table.

underframe for table
with thumb screws

underframe for table
assembled as a unit

Fig. 47   Tripod table – underside of the top.

VICTORIAN EXTENDING DINING TABLES

The Victorian extending table is made up of two sections, each of which consists of a top that is attached to one end and two siderails. The rails themselves are mortise and tenoned into two legs at one end, and the two separate sections of table are joined together by sliding rails fitted into grooves on the inside of the siderails. The greater the number of slides, the greater the number of leaves that can be inserted.

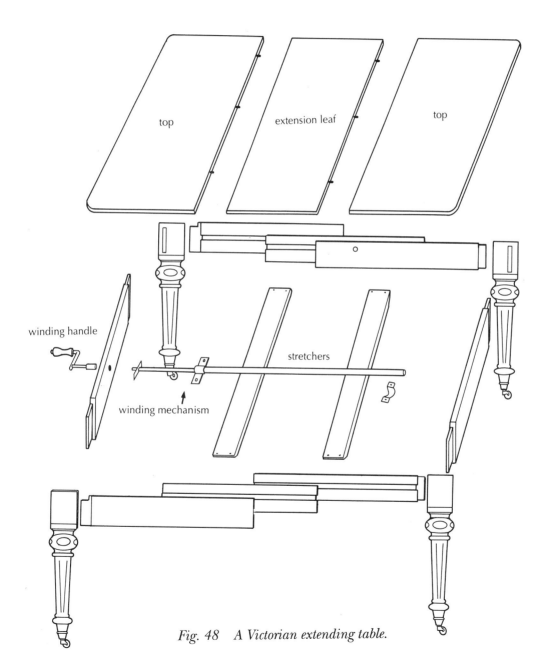

top

extension leaf

top

winding handle

stretchers

winding mechanism

Fig. 48   A Victorian extending table.

The sliding rails are kept in place in the grooves by stretchers fitted between them which prevent them from coming out of the groove as the table is extended. Extension of the table is achieved either by pulling the two sections apart, or in some cases by means of a winding mechanism.

It is possible to unscrew the stretchers from between the slides and, with the table at its full extension, ease the slides out of the grooves and separate the table into its two sections. In the case of the wind-out, of course, it will be necessary to detach the winding mechanism.

The table top is attached to the rails with screws, some of which are only accessible when the table is fully extended.

CARD AND SUPPER TABLES

Card and supper tables can be split into two types, as far as their tops are concerned. They may have the top fitted with either screws or glue blocks as any other table, in which case the top would open up and be supported on fly or gate legs at the rear. Alternatively, they may be fitted with a single nut and bolt, about which the top will swivel and open up to be supported on the underframe. The biggest problem with this type of table is often that the card table hinges, securing the two halves of the top. These screws often have very little slot left in the top and need drilling and removing with a screw extractor. For this reason the tops are best left joined unless absolutely necessary.

The bases of these tables can be of the conventional type with four legs, in which case they can be treated as a normal table, or they can be on a pillar base (see tripod tables, above).

REMOVING NAILS FROM JOINTS

The only truly successful way to repair a joint is to take it apart, clean off any old glue, and reglue it. Unfortunately many joints have at some time been 'repaired' by having a nail put through them. This may in the short term stop the joint from coming apart, but it does not stop any movement in the joint and will in due course cause damage. It also makes it far more difficult to take the joint apart to carry out a proper repair. In fact, once a joint has been nailed, some damage is inevitable. The nail has to come out before any attempt is made to separate the joint. This is accomplished by securing the leg or rail in a vice and drilling a hole approximately the same diameter as the nail to one side of it. Try to feel your way down the side of the nail and make sure you drill all the way to the bottom. When this has been done, tap the nail head over into the hole you have just drilled by using a small nail punch and drill another hole on the other side of the nail. It should now be possible to grip the nail with a pair of pointed pliers and extract it. Once the nail is out it should then be a simple job to separate the joint.

The above course of action is easy in the telling, but requires some practice and I would advise that you try removing some nails from a piece of waste timber before you try it on an antique. Remember it is necessary to follow the nail with the drill all the way to the bottom.

REMOVING OLD SCREWS

Screws which have been in place for some time can be very difficult to remove. The usual consequence of the inexperienced person trying to do so is that the screw shank or head breaks under the strain of the attempt. Always be sure you have a screwdriver of the correct size and in good order. Ensure that the slot of the screw is clean and tap the head of the screwdriver with a hammer to ensure a snug fit. Before attempting to undo the screw try doing it up. Although this may sound silly, it really does work, as the pressures on the screw are more even when being done up. What normally happens when a screw breaks is that it is just the tip of the screw which is held fast, so when you start to undo it the shank twists and breaks. Doing the screw up usually avoids this, and once it is moving and the tip is free it can be removed normally.

It is also a good idea to fill the screw hole with a soft wood such as poplar, to ensure the screw will do up tight when replaced.

REMOVING WOODEN PEGS

Wooden pegs were used on early oak furniture, both for securing mortise and tenon joints and as a means of attaching tops. These pegs, although driven into round holes, were in fact square in section, split with the grain. Examining these pegs to see if they are round or square in section is one thing to do when trying to determine if a piece is antique or reproduction, or if a genuine piece has been repaired or altered. If the pegs are round on the ends, then they, at least, are new. Genuine old pegs are always square and always slightly proud of the surface, never flush.

Usually the pegs go all the way through and can easily be tapped out from the other side. If this is not the case then they will have to be drilled out. The method of drilling out pegs is the same as that used for removing dowels and is explained in that section of Chapter 5. It is necessary to employ this method because the pegs will

not be entirely straight, due to the way they were fitted. A hole was first drilled through the mortise without the tenon in place, then the tenon was inserted and the position of the hole marked on the tenon. The joint was then taken apart and a hole drilled in the tenon slightly off-centre so that the action of driving the peg home would pull the joint together. Because of this the pegs are always misshapen.

RELEASING OLD GLUE

Usually, if a joint will not come apart easily with a tap from a large hammer, as described in the section on dismantling, I would suggest that the joint is left well alone, and the repair, whatever it may be, carried out in some other way. However, the occasion may arise when it will be necessary to separate a glued block or joint that is not loose, and which cannot easily be knocked apart without risking damage. In this case some method of loosening the adhesive will have to be found.

Animal glues can be softened with water, heat or methylated spirits. It must be remembered, however, that all three of these agents can and will damage polished surfaces. Gentle heat is the safest to use on joints, but as a last resort you can drill a fine hole into the cavity at the base of the joint and inject the methylated spirits. The meths will not react immediately, especially if the joint is a tight fit.

Modern glues can most often be loosened with methylated spirits, polyurethane thinners, white spirit, turpentine or Nitromors paint remover, all of which will damage polished surfaces. Remember to use all chemicals in a well-ventilated area and to protect your eyes.

CHAPTER five

Repairs to parts of furniture

JOINTS

DOWEL JOINT

If a dowel joint becomes loose it has to be reglued along the whole length of the dowel. All too often, when the dowel joint is knocked apart, it is assumed that if the dowel stays in one side of the joint then that part of the joint must still be strong. Nothing could be further from the truth. If, for instance, we are talking about a joint between a leg and a seat rail, then the dowel is glued into both the leg and the rail at the same time, under the same conditions, and with the same glue. When the joint is knocked apart the dowel will naturally stay in the rail, because in the rail it will not be in contact with any end grain and so the bond will be marginally stronger than in the leg. However, the dowel must be changed, if the repair is not to be repeated within a few months. Sometimes the dowel can be removed by placing the rail in a vice, gripping the dowel with a pair of pinchers or pliers and hammering the pliers upwards. I recommend that an old or cheap pair of pliers be kept for this purpose. If, however, this does not remove the dowel very easily then it should be cut off flush with the end of the rail and drilled out. It is a mistake to try and drill a dowel out in one go with a drill bit of the same diameter as the dowel, as it is almost impossible to follow the line and angle of the dowel exactly and, unless this is done, great difficulty will be experienced when reassembling the item of furniture.

A hole approximately two-thirds the diameter of the dowel should be drilled in the centre of the dowel. This hole must be drilled all the way to the bottom of the dowel, but no further. This may sound difficult, but after a little practice you will soon be able to feel when the bottom of the dowel is reached, as there is invariably a gap filled with glue at the base of the dowel. When this has been accomplished the dowel must be prised away from the edge of the dowel hole. This is best done by tapping a small bradawl or other pointed implement between the wall of the hole and the dowel. The bradawl must be pointed, but not sharp – if it is sharp, it will simply dig into the wood and not follow the joint between the dowel proper and the wall of the dowel hole. The dowel can then be removed in slivers with a pair of pointed pliers. Sometimes it will be found that after the first sliver of dowel is removed, the rest of the dowel can be removed in one piece.

When the new dowel is cut for the joint it should be cut slightly short of the depth of the two holes. This is to ensure that the shoulders of the joint make firm contact when the joint is assembled, and are not kept apart by the dowel being too long. The sides of the dowel should be scored with glue grooves to enable the glue to ooze out of the joint when it is assembled, and the end should be chamfered.

If it is necessary to remark and redrill a dowel hole – for instance, if the rail has been made new, or if the end has been spliced, it is important to check whether the pieces to be dowelled together fit flush or are stepped.

It is an easy matter when making a new

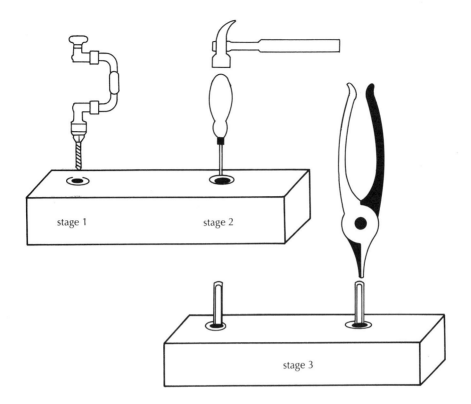

Fig. 49   Removing a dowel.

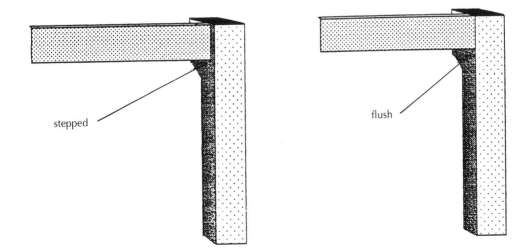

Fig. 50   Flush and stepped joints.

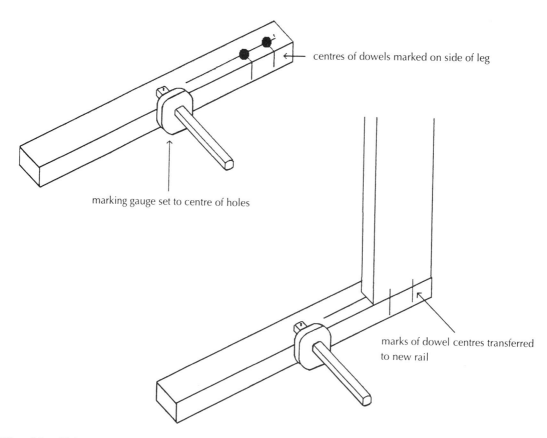

centres of dowels marked on side of leg

marking gauge set to centre of holes

marks of dowel centres transferred to new rail

Fig. 51   Using a marking gauge to position dowel holes.

piece of furniture to mark and drill the dowels, as a marking gauge can be set and used on both pieces to be joined. It is not such an easy matter, however, when you already have the holes in one piece and you have to mark the other to match.

One method I have found helpful is to stick masking tape on the side of the piece with the original holes, then take a square and square across from the centre of the hole as accurately as possible and mark this centre on the masking tape. You can then hold the new piece in position and transfer the mark across. All you have to do then is set your gauge as near as possible to the centre of the hole and transfer this mark onto your new work. Mark the position of the hole carefully

and then drill a pilot hole, with a small bit. Re-check the positions and then drill with the correct size bit. Be sure to check the angle at which the dowel is drilled, as it may not be parallel with the sides of the leg.

Another method of marking which may be possible if you are marking a new piece of wood, and the dowel has been cut off in the other section, is to hammer a panel pin into the centre of the cut-off dowel, snip off the end of the pin, leaving it proud, and then file it to a point. Assemble the joint dry and the sharpened end of the pin will mark the position of the new hole. The pin can then be removed and the dowel extracted as described.

KNUCKLE JOINT

The knuckle joint is a joint that acts like a hinge. Two pieces of wood are castellated at the ends so that they fit together, and are held together in this manner by a metal rod, around which they pivot. This type of joint is most often found on the leaf supports of Pembroke and sofa tables.

The most common reason for repair of these joints is wear. After many years of use they become loose and sloppy in operation, and the hole through which the metal rod passes becomes enlarged. In order to carry out a successful repair the joint will have to be dismantled. It may be possible to extract the metal rod without removing the top of the table, if enough of it is projecting from the bottom of the joint to be grasped with pliers. Failing this, the table top will have to be removed and the rod tapped out with a fine nail punch. The problem of an enlarged hole can normally be solved by inserting a slightly larger-diameter rod when reassembling. However, if the wear is too great to be solved in this way, the holes will have to be filled with wood and re-drilled. Any wear

between the knuckles themselves will have to be made up by making sure the surfaces are flat and gluing on extra wood or veneer to make up the gap.

Sometimes you will need to replace part or all of a joint, either because it is badly wormed or because at some time the metal rod has dropped out, allowing the joint to separate and part of it to be misplaced.

The first thing to be done when making a replacement joint is to select a suitable piece of timber and cut and plane it to size, allowing enough length for the knuckles to fit together and for any mortise and tenon. Set a marking gauge to mark the middle of the timber and draw two circles on the top edge either side of a line where the joint is to be cut, but not quite touching it.

Square the line around the timber and also the centres of the circles. Draw the two circles on the bottom edge of the timber. The next operation is to drill a fine hole through the centres of the circles. This has to be very accurate, and I have found that the best way to achieve a good result is to start with a fine bit and drill half-way in from each end. Once the first fine holes have been drilled, drill again using a

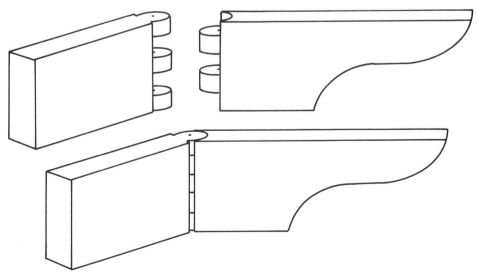

Fig. 52   A knuckle joint.

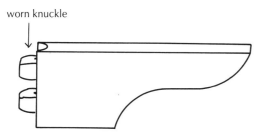
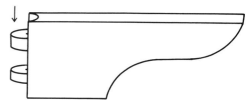
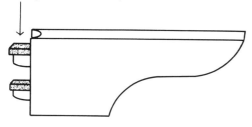
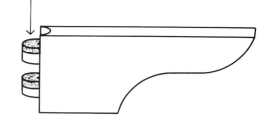

worn knuckle

worn sections cut away

new wood glued on to make up for wear

new wood shaped and drilled

Fig. 53   Making good a worn knuckle joint.

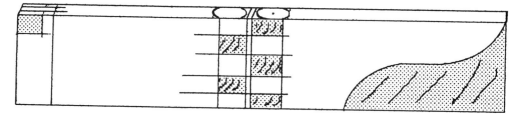

Fig. 54   Marking out a replacement knuckle joint.

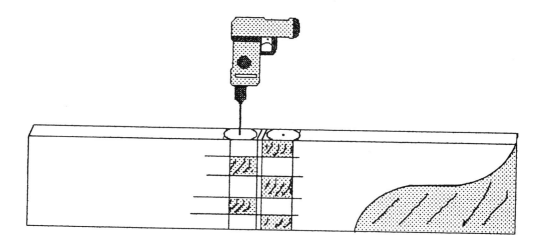

Fig. 55   Drilling the joint.

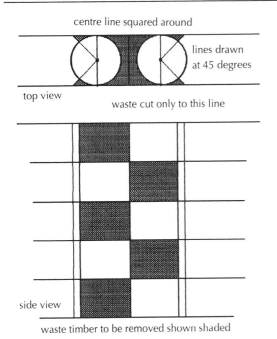

centre line squared around

lines drawn at 45 degrees

top view

waste cut only to this line

side view

waste timber to be removed shown shaded

Fig. 56   Marking out the knuckles.

slightly larger bit and continue in this way until you are using the correct size bit for the diameter of the rod.

The next job is to mark out the knuckles themselves. If you are only replacing one part of the joint it will of course be necessary to mark them using the existing half; if not, then you should refer to the other joints on the table. First, draw a line at 45 degrees from the centre of the circles to the edge of the timber. Where this line crosses the circumference of the circle, a line is drawn square to the edge of the timber, and this line should be squared down. When you cut the waste timber out of the knuckle you must only cut to this new line.

The next job to be done is to remove the waste timber from between the knuckles so that they fit together. This involves rounding the ends and hollowing out between the knuckles to correspond with the circumferences of the circles. This must be done so that when the two halves of the joint are assembled the holes in each section line up exactly. When the joint fits

together and the holes line up, it is possible to cut and shape the fly-rail and cut any tenon that is required. Only when all this has been accomplished should you think of inserting the metal rod. After the rod has been inserted it will be possible to carry out fine adjustments to the joint, ensuring that the round knuckles present an even appearance. At this stage when the joint is operated it will not open to its full extent because of the square shoulders. These shoulders should now be chamfered to allow the joint full movement.

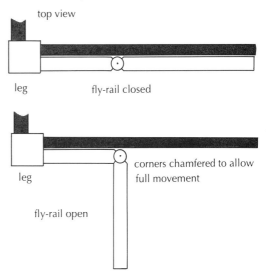

top view

leg   fly-rail closed

leg

corners chamfered to allow full movement

fly-rail open

Fig. 57   The finished knuckle joint.

MORTISE AND TENON JOINT

The mortise

The most common problem found with a mortise is where it is near the end of a rail or leg which has split. This usually occurs because the joint has been loose for some time and has gone unrepaired. This problem is very common with the tops of front chair legs, and it is often the case that just regluing will not be a strong enough repair. If this is the case then it may be necessary to splice the end of the leg and cut a new mortise.

bottom of original mortise

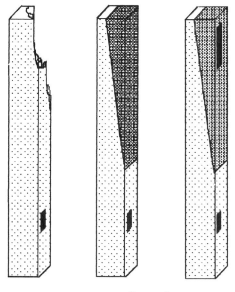

note distance between joints

Fig. 58   Splicing the end of a chair leg to cut a new mortise.

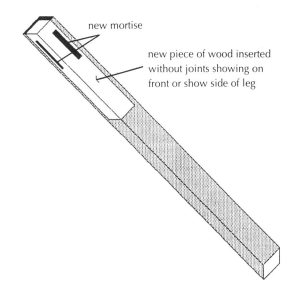

new mortise

new piece of wood inserted without joints showing on front or show side of leg

Fig. 59   Letting in a concealed mortise repair.

If the top of the leg is being cut in such a way that the position of the mortise is lost, it is important to mark the position of the mortise before cutting, even though the other leg may be available as a guide. One way of doing this is to put some masking tape lower down on the leg, and mark a line on it a predetermined distance from one end of the mortise. A mortise gauge can also be preset before cutting, and in this way it should prove no problem to re-mark the mortise on the new timber in exactly the right place. Always study the leg carefully before cutting to determine the best way to splice: it may be possible to avoid having any of the joint showing on the front of the leg at all. If both the front and show side of the leg are intact, it may even be possible to let in a suitable piece of wood entirely from the back of the leg.

The tenon

With tenon repairs there are several options open to the restorer, depending on the severity of the damage. It may be

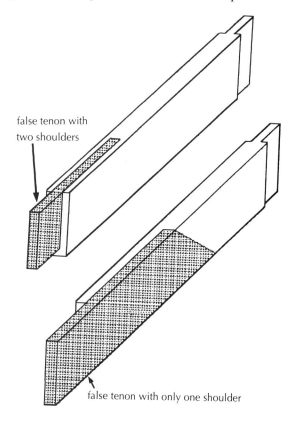

false tenon with two shoulders

false tenon with only one shoulder

Fig. 60   A false tenon.

that the end of the rail will need to be spliced the same as when repairing a mortise, but one very useful option is to make what is known as a false tenon. This is where a section of the centre of the rail is cut away, almost as if it were a large mortise, and a new piece of wood inserted. This piece of wood is left long enough for a new tenon to be cut on the end. If the tenon is in the middle of the rail, any repair carried out this way should only be detectable from underneath. Sometimes, however, especially with seat rails, it will be found that the tenon is not in the middle of the rail and that there is only a shoulder on one side. When this is the case a false tenon can still be used, but the new piece of wood will have to be let in on the inside of the rail. Even though this type of repair is unobtrusive, never be tempted to use inferior wood – always choose a matching piece of timber for strength.

CHAIR RAIL JOINTS

Sometimes a rail in a chair may be loose,

but it cannot be removed for regluing because the other rails are holding fast. In these circumstances great care is needed. It is best if the joint can be opened a little to allow for the insertion of some glue through a bore hole. The rail is placed in the vice as if for dismantling and the joint is carefully knocked apart, sufficient only to expose the very start of the tenon. This can normally be done if the offending rail is not too close to any other. A small hole is drilled into the mortise through the exposed tenon, glue is inserted with a syringe, and the joint cramped back together. When the joint is together there should be no sign of the bore hole. If it has not been possible to spring the joint in that way because of the proximity of other rails, then a small bore hole must be drilled into the mortise from elsewhere. Usually this can be done unobtrusively underneath the rail and a small wooden plug inserted into the hole after glue has been injected. If it has not been possible to open the joint at all then it is difficult to predict how successful the repair will be. Never be tempted to use a dowel, or worse still a nail,

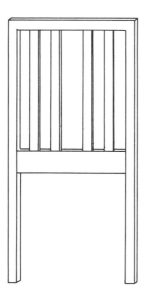

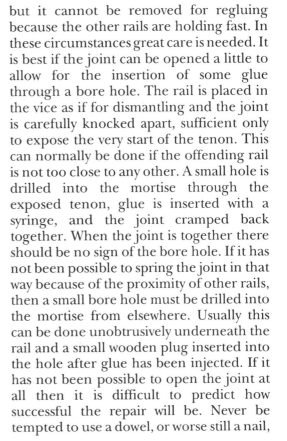

glue injected into
partially
open joint

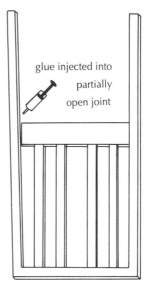

Fig. 61   Regluing a chair-rail joint.

as this will only cause more problems in the future. Far better to leave well alone until another joint becomes loose, when a more satisfactory repair can be carried out.

DRAWERS

There are certain variations in the method of drawer construction: the older type has the grain of the bottom board running from front to back and the more recent type has the grain running from side to side. Both types of drawer usually have the sides dovetailed to the front and back (see Fig. 42), but in the older type of drawer the sides are housed at the bottom to take the bottom boards, which are glued or nailed in place and then have a runner glued on top. The later type is basically the same, except the bottom boards are chamfered at the sides and are fitted into grooves in the drawer sides. The runners

are then glued onto the drawer bottom, up against the drawer side. With drawers made after about 1830 the bottoms were fitted into dust strips which were glued on the inside of the drawer.

The most common repair needed for drawers is replacement of worn runners. When the drawer runners are badly worn, damage can then be caused to the drawer fronts or to the front stiles of the cabinet, due to veneers or cock-beading catching as the drawer is slid in and out.

If it is found on examination of the drawer that there are loose dovetail joints, then these will have to be dealt with before any repairs to runners can commence. If the drawer runners are of the dust-strip type and are not being changed, it should be possible to knock apart the offending joint and reglue with no difficulty.

With drawers prior to 1830 where there is no dust strip, the old drawer runners will have to be carefully removed with a

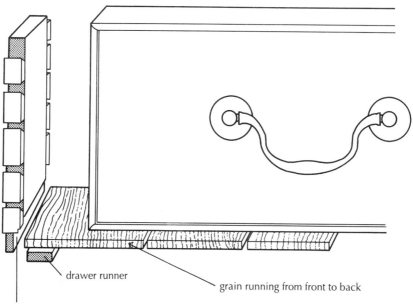

drawer runner

grain running from front to back

rebate in drawer side for bottom boards

Fig. 62   An older-type drawer.

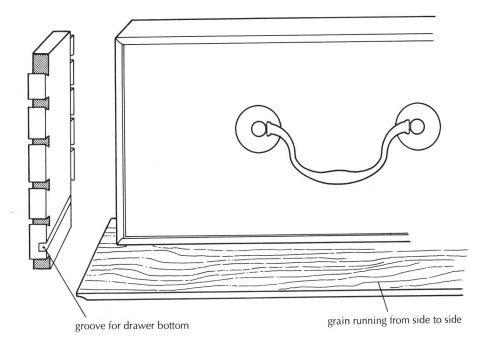

groove for drawer bottom

grain running from side to side

Fig. 63   A later-type drawer.

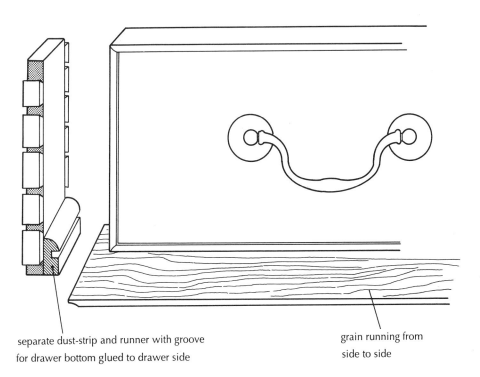

separate dust-strip and runner with groove
for drawer bottom glued to drawer side

grain running from
side to side

Fig. 64   Drawer with separate dust strips.

hammer and chisel, after first cutting with a tenon saw between the drawer side and the runner. This is done to avoid damaging the drawer side. A new piece of wood can then be fitted. This is best held in place with springs while the glue dries (see Chapter 11 on cramping). The new drawer runner should, when fitted, be left proud of the drawer front until the glue is dry and then carefully planed down just enough to allow the drawer to fit into its space. The top of the drawer front should fit snug against the stile above it, without rubbing. Sometimes, in extremely bad cases the wear is so bad that the side of the drawer has to be repaired as well. In this case it will be necessary to take the drawer apart and replace part of the drawer side first.

Remember to check the condition of the runners and guides in the cabinet itself – these may need replacing as well.

Another repair which is sometimes necessary is to make good any gaps which form between the bottom boards of a drawer because of shrinkage. With drawers which have the grain running from front to back, it is simply a matter of cutting and gluing in strips of matching timber. The problem that arises with drawers that have the grain running from side to side is where the bottom no longer fits into the groove in the drawer front. The solution to this is to remove the screws or cut the nails securing the bottom to the drawer back and move the drawer bottom forward into the groove and refix. It may in some cases be necessary to glue a piece of matching timber on the back edge of the drawer bottom, to make up for the shrinkage.

SEQUENCE OF REPAIRS

1.   Does the drawer need to come apart? Remember, it may be possible to get away with just replacing the runners if the drawer sides are not badly worn. Repairs to the drawer front can usually be undertaken with the drawer intact.

2.   If the drawer has to come apart, do the runners have to be removed before the drawer bottom, or is the bottom fitted into a dust strip?

3.   Has the side of the drawer worn to the extent that it needs to be built up?

4.   Remember when regluing that it is the drawer bottom to a large extent which holds the drawer square, and if any repairs have been carried out on it, it is a good idea to check that it is still square with the cabinet, before refitting. This is done by sliding the drawer bottom into its position in the cabinet, holding it against the drawer guide on one side and seeing if the front of the drawer bottom is parallel to the front of the cabinet, adjusting it if not.

If the drawer runners on the drawers themselves are worn, it may well be that the runners in the cabinet also need repairing or replacing. On Victorian furniture these runners are often fitted into rebates in the cabinet side and have a small tongue fitting into a groove on the back of the front stile. Often on early chests they are simply glued to the cabinet side. Mark well the position of the runners before removing them. They not only form a runner for the drawer that rests on them, but they also prevent the drawer below from dropping when it is pulled out. The runners have to be an equal distance apart, front and back, or the drawer will jam.

NEW DRAWER SIDE

If it is necessary to completely replace a drawer side for one reason or another, then you should be able to use the opposite side as a template, provided of course that

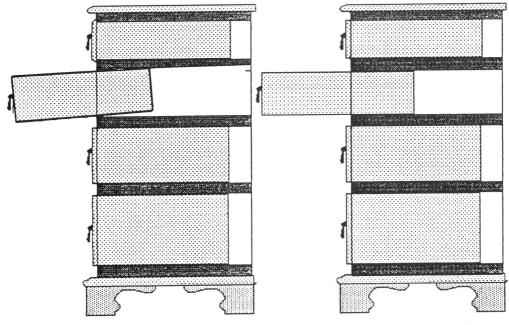

badly fitted runner allows drawer to drop   correctly fitted runner prevents drawer dropping

Fig. 65   How the drawer runners work.

it is not in need of similar treatment too. If both sides need to be replaced and completely new dovetails marked, have a good look at the dovetails of other drawers from the cabinet to see how they are spaced and how many there are. Remember, of course, that, if you do use an existing drawer side as a template, any groove or rebate will have to be on the opposite side, and also remember to allow for any wear that has been suffered by the drawer side which you are using for a template. Cut the piece of wood for the new drawer side to just fit into its position in the chest or cabinet and then lay the opposite side on top of it to mark the dovetails front and rear. It is often a good idea when you have cut the new side to size to run it into its place in the chest and check that the front of it is parallel with the front of the chest – far better to discover any discrepancy at this stage rather than discover that the drawer front leans in or out after it has been glued. If a whole new drawer is being made, it is a good idea to pin the sides together when cutting the dovetail joints to ensure these are cut exactly the same both sides.

NEW DRAWER FRONT

If it is necessary to replace a drawer front, the new front must be cut and planed to fit the cabinet before the joints are cut. Remember that not all antique cabinets are perfectly square, and nothing looks worse than a drawer that doesn't fit its space. The new joints can then be cut normally by using the dovetails of the drawer side as a template.

NEW DRAWER BOTTOM

When the bottom of a new drawer is made it should be square with the front of the cabinet. This way, when the drawer is glued up, the drawer bottom, if properly fitted,

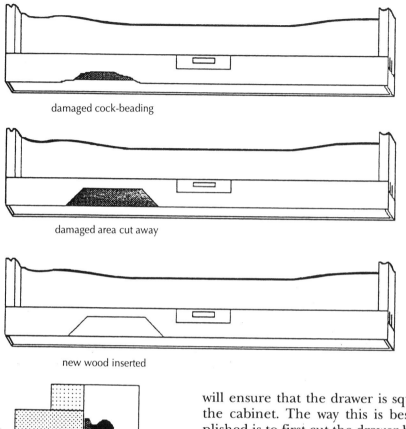

damaged cock-beading

damaged area cut away

new wood inserted

fine adjustment of the new piece of cock-beading
using a shooting block and smoothing plane

Fig. 66   Replacing damaged cock-beading.

will ensure that the drawer is square with the cabinet. The way this is best accomplished is to first cut the drawer bottom to the correct width and then slide it into the chest, holding it against the drawer guide on one side and marking with a pencil underneath along the front rail.

COCK-BEADING

Any cock-beading which is damaged can be cut away and replaced with a new piece of wood which is glued in place on the top and bottom edges of the drawer, and glued and nailed on the sides, where it is on end grain. When dry it is planed flush with the rest of the beading and shaped with a scraper. The best way to ensure a good joint when fitting cock-beading is to cut the joints where the new butts against the old on an angle. They can then be adjusted to fit by planing them on a shooting block; minute adjustment is possible using this method.

REPLACING CHAIR RAILS

Sometimes it is necessary to replace a rail without dismantling the piece of furniture in question. This is often the case with the back seat rails of chairs, when the rail in question is beech and has been badly affected by worm. If the other joints on the chair are solid and it is not possible to take them apart, the rail can still be replaced.

The first thing that has to be done is to cut a new piece of wood for the rail. This should be the same height as the original and long enough to include the tenons, but it should be left a saw cut's thickness thicker than the original rail. Measure and mark the shoulders of the new tenons accurately – it will not, of course, be possible to mark the tenons themselves until the old rail has been removed and the mortises exposed. Carefully cut through the old rail as near as possible to the ends, without the danger of marking the chair with the saw. Once this has been done the old tenons must be carefully cleaned out of the mortises. This is best done by drilling them first with the aid of a flexible chuck and then cleaning out with a small chisel. When this has been accomplished it will be possible to mark the new tenons on the new rail and cut them.

Now that the new rail exists, the only problem is in fitting it. This is accomplished by cutting the new rail from the back shoulder at one end to the front shoulder at the other. It should now be possible to glue the new rail in place in two separate pieces. This type of repair is not limited to chairs – the principle can be used to replace any rail where it is not possible to dismantle the piece of furniture.

LEGS
SQUARE LEG REPAIRS

The vulnerable part of a square or tapered leg is normally at the top, around the joints. This is because a square leg is inherently strong and the main cause of damage is the joint becoming loose through the glue drying out. When the joint is loose and there is movement in the leg, there is a good chance that the leg will split near the joint. If the leg is only slightly split it may be possible to open the split a little, get some glue into the split and cramp until dry. However, if the leg is badly broken, it may be necessary to splice on a new piece of wood and recut the mortises. (See Mortise and tenon joint, above.)

If the leg is of plain, solid timber it can simply be cut as shown in Fig. 58 and a piece of similar timber glued on (see Chapter 11 on cramping). This new piece of wood is

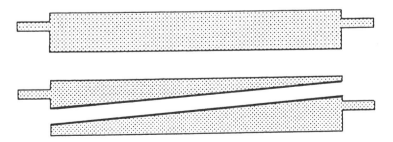

seat rail cut in two from shoulder to shoulder so that it can be fitted without dismantling the chair

Fig. 67   Method for replacing a chair rail.

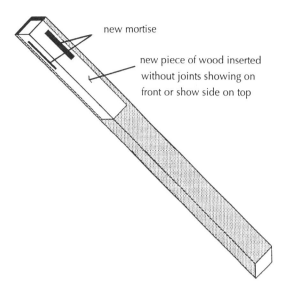

new mortise

new piece of wood inserted without joints showing on front or show side on top

Fig. 68   Concealed repair to a square leg.

planed to size when the glue is dry and then any new joints can be cut. If the leg is not so plain, however, and has some form of decoration on it – for example, veneer or carving – then you have two options. You can either cut off the decoration from the front of the leg, repair or replace the leg and re-apply the decoration, or you can splice a new piece on the leg and make up whatever decoration is lost. In the case of veneer, of course, and especially marquetry, keeping the original intact is of the utmost importance. Each case must be considered on its merits, and it is sometimes possible, of course, to insert a new piece of wood without touching the outer sides.

Any splice on a leg has to be very strong: most chairs will be called upon to support somebody's weight. This means that the joint has to be as long as possible, to give the maximum possible gluing surface. A

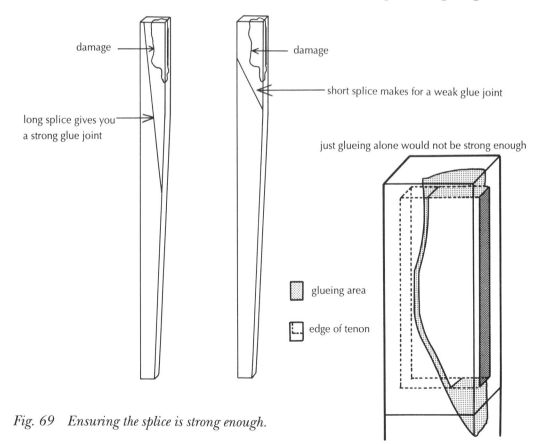

damage

long splice gives you a strong glue joint

damage

short splice makes for a weak glue joint

just glueing alone would not be strong enough

glueing area

edge of tenon

Fig. 69   Ensuring the splice is strong enough.

short splice will have only a small gluing area and will mean more end grain. A longer splice will have a larger gluing area and will be more long grain.

DOWELLING A TURNED LEG

It is an unfortunate fact that, because most turnings have sections of varying thicknesses, and consequently varying strength, they will invariably break across the grain at the weakest point. For this reason it is seldom possible to repair a turning by regluing alone. Some method of strengthening will almost certainly be needed, and a dowel is the most obvious candidate. If the break is not too far from one end, it may be possible to simply reglue the leg or pillar, allow to dry and then drill and dowel from one end well past the area of damage. If for one reason or another this is not practical, then the following method should be employed.

Drill one section of the damaged leg only. This should be done at first with a small pilot bit, building up to a bit approximately two-thirds the diameter of the narrowest part of the leg. Every care should be taken to avoid damaging the fibres of the damaged end, as the better these knit back with the other half, the less the repair will show. When the first section has been drilled, the damaged end of this section can then be cut off at the nearest convenient point and glued onto the other section of turning, taking care to ensure the fibres fit together correctly. When the glue has dried the second section can be drilled and the holes should line up.

Sometimes it is the square section at the top of a leg which becomes damaged, where the mortise and tenon joints are. If this is the case and it is necessary to make a new piece, the new square top section can be put onto a lathe and have a dowel turned on one end.

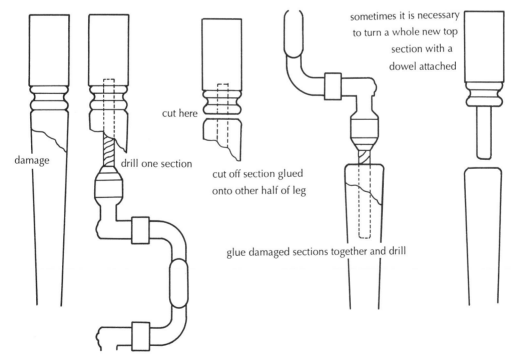

damage

drill one section

cut here

cut off section glued onto other half of leg

glue damaged sections together and drill

sometimes it is necessary to turn a whole new top section with a dowel attached

Fig. 70   Repairing a turned leg.

six

Repairs to damaged turning

WOODTURNING

The lathe is unique amongst wood-working machines. All other woodworking machines – for mortising, planing, sawing, carving and so on – have been made to do a job that was previously done by hand. But without a lathe, woodturning is impossible. It has been made to do a job that could not otherwise be done – you can't turn by hand.

The basic chisels used for wood-turning are the gouge and the side chisel, which are used for cutting – that is to say, they are held at an angle to the work so that they cut shavings, and are generally used with a lateral sliding movement, left or right. The other chisels are used for scraping, that is that they approach the work in a more or less horizontal position.

As with any aspect of woodworking, sharp tools are essential in woodturning. The tool rest must be positioned as near as possible to the work and the chisel held firmly. Some people like to have a hand on top of the chisel where it crosses the tool rest, others like to grip the chisel between finger and thumb and support the index finger against the tool rest. You must decide which is most comfortable for you. Remember that in woodturning, as

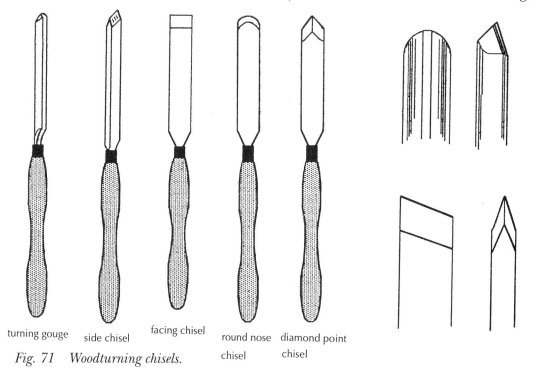

turning gouge   side chisel   facing chisel   round nose chisel   diamond point chisel

Fig. 71   Woodturning chisels.

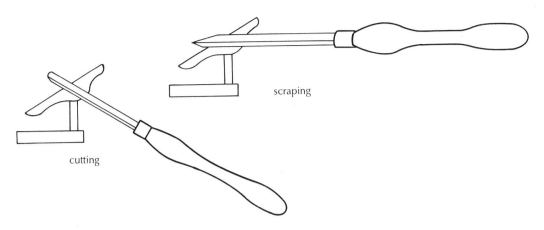

Fig. 72   Cutting and scraping.

with all woodwork, it is *not* a good idea to cut against the grain. Always cut from the high part of the turning towards the low.

Most repairs to damaged turnings can be dealt with by regluing the break, or by turning a new section and dowelling it onto the original at a convenient point in the turning. Occasionally, however, it may be necessary to splice a new piece of timber onto the turning, as if one was repairing a square leg, and then to fit the whole thing onto a lathe and turn the new part. This presents us with quite a problem, as, although it is possible that the old end will still have the centre visible where it was originally fitted on a lathe, the new end will have to have a centre marked very accurately so as not to throw the old turning off-centre. The best method I have found of achieving this is to fit the old centre in place on the head end of the lathe and then position the tailstock against the new end with enough pressure to just hold it lightly in place. Position the tool rest as if for turning, hold a pencil against the old turning at a point as near the tailstock as possible and slowly rotate the lathe manually. As the turning rotates it will alternately push the pencil away and move back away from it. With a small hammer you can lightly tap the end of the turning

at the tailstock to alter its position. Continue to adjust the position of the new end in this manner until the pencil is in contact with the old turning throughout a whole rotation of the work (see Fig 73).

PILLARS

Pillars and pedestals can in general be treated in the same way as turned legs. One of the more common problems encountered is with the bases of tripod tables. These often come to grief at the point where the legs are attached by means of slot dovetails. If undue weight or pressure is put on the table, then the shoulders of the slot can split and break away. Sometimes it is possible to glue them back and even reinforce them with small hardwood dowels, but if, as is often the case, they have been unsuccessfully repaired before, it may be necessary to turn a new bottom section and cut new joints. The new section should be turned with a suitable dowel on it (see Fig 74).

CABRIOLE LEGS

Replacing a cabriole leg is more a job for

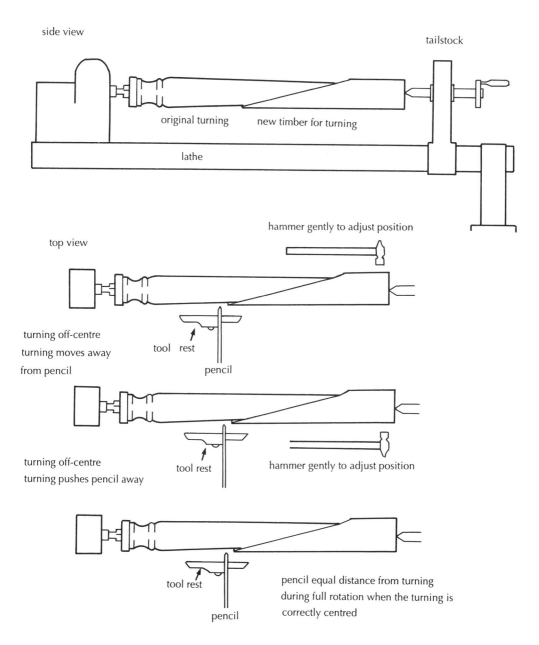

Fig. 73   Positioning a spliced repair for turning.

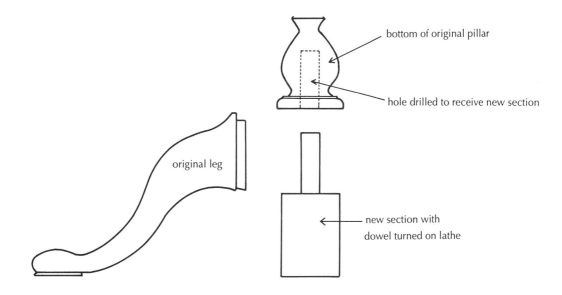

Fig. 74   Replacement section for pillar repair.

a carver than for a cabinet-maker but, as a true restorer has to be both these things and more, I will give a brief description of the basic technique. However, a good eye and some experience of carving are essential if this is to be undertaken well.

The very first thing to be done when replacing a shaped leg poses an immediate problem. It will be necessary to make a template of the old leg or another leg from the cabinet or chair. Stiff cartridge paper is the best medium to use. Hold the paper against the leg and draw around it as accurately as possible and cut out the shape. Because of the contours of the leg, when the template is laid out flat it will be longer than the original leg and the shape consequently distorted. This can't be helped.

Next, select the timber from which the new leg is to be made. Careful measurements must be taken from the original and the new timber cut to size, remembering to make allowances for any carving at the knee or foot. Mark accurately the top and bottom of the leg. Place your template on the timber with the top of the template

level with the mark for the top of the leg. Draw around your template with a pencil, but do not mark all the way to the bottom. Then move the template down until the bottom of it is level with the bottom of the leg, again mark around your template, but this time do not mark all the way to the top. At this stage you will have the top and bottom of the leg marked on the new timber but the line marking the centre of the leg will overlap. The junction of these two sets of marks will have to be joined free-hand to match the shape of the original leg. When you are confident that the drawing you have on the wood is a good match to the original leg, the shape can be cut out on a bandsaw. This must be done carefully and the waste offcuts must be saved.

The next stage is to place the template once again on the timber, but this time against the cut section. If the previous measurings and drawings have been accurate, the template should be the right length when held against the contours just cut. This shape can now be cut out on the bandsaw. It will be necessary to replace

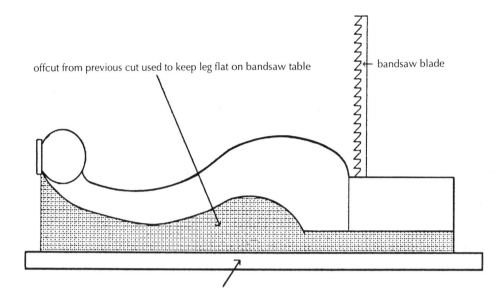

offcut from previous cut used to keep leg flat on bandsaw table

bandsaw blade

Fig. 75   Cutting on the bandsaw.

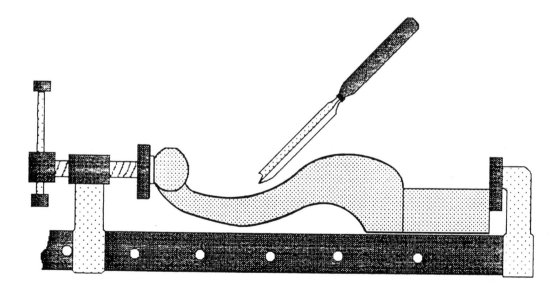

Fig. 76   Shaping the cut leg.

the offcuts from the previous cut, in order to hold the work flat on the bandsaw table.

You should now have a square cabriole leg the same dimensions as the original, allowing for any carved decoration. If the dimensions do not correspond in one place or another, now is the time to correct it. When you are happy with the overall size and shape of the new leg, the process of shaping and carving can begin. The leg can be held in a sash cramp for shaping with a spoke shave or chisel. Keep checking dimensions with a pair of callipers – have the original leg at hand so that shape and general appearance can be constantly checked.

seven

Repairing splits

SPLIT TOPS

Splits in the top of a table or any other cabinet can be very difficult to repair successfully, unless the split is straight. If the top is veneered into the bargain, the task may seem insurmountable. No problem is beyond solution, however, even if a new top has to be made, but the question that has to be asked is how far to go. If the split is quite small and not too unsightly, perhaps all that needs to be done is to inlay a small dovetail key in the underside to prevent the split from getting any worse. This can be a very successful repair on both veneered and solid tops, provided of course that the underside is not visible, as would be the case with the top of a foldover supper or tea table. If a dovetail key is a viable solution then it should be cut from a hard wood such as mahogany and inlaid to a depth of at least half the thickness of the top, and preferably two-thirds. When marking out the dovetail, do not angle the sides too steeply as this will leave vulnerable points at the corners. It is far better to have a gentle slope, which means that you have less short grain and a stronger dovetail.

When chopping out the dovetail you must remember that you will be close to the top surface. The best thing to do is to mark on a metal drill bit the depth you intend to go. This can quite easily be done with a piece of masking tape. Mark the outline of your dovetail on the work and drill several holes inside the area to the correct depth. This means that there will be far less hammering to do. However, it will still be

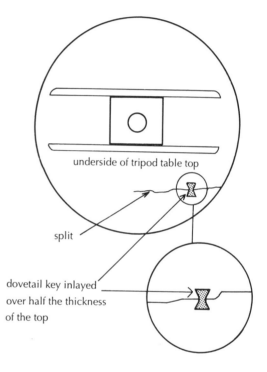

underside of tripod table top

split

dovetail key inlayed over half the thickness of the top

Fig. 77   A dovetail repair.

prudent to cramp a suitable block of wood on the opposite side, to support the work.

Sometimes the split in the top is no more than a joint between two planks opening up, due to shrinkage or the drying out of glue. In this case, if the top is of solid timber, it is best if the split can be continued right across the top and then for the top to be rejointed. If this is not possible a dovetail key may be the best option. If it is possible to continue the split and separate the two planks, it will be necessary to plane the joint with a try-plane in order to get a perfect fit for rejointing.

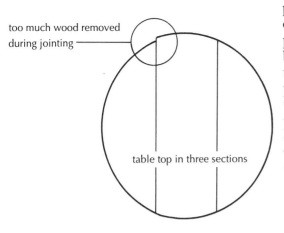

too much wood removed during jointing

table top in three sections

tops closed like a book for planing

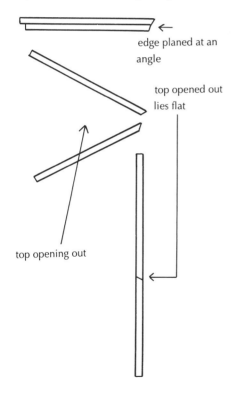

edge planed at an angle

top opened out lies flat

top opening out

Fig. 78   A rejointing repair.

Care must be taken to ensure that the minimum amount of wood is removed – this is especially the case with round or oval tops.

When planing a joint between two planks of wood, whether for the first time or when rejointing a split top, the two pieces should be closed up as if closing a book and cramped together. Ensure that the two edges are as parallel and flush as possible, and plane a straight edge on them together. In this way, even if they are planed at an angle, when they are opened out again they will lie flat. It is important when making this type of joint to use a try-plane, so that a very straight edge can be obtained.

Where you have a split which is not straight and which will not close together with cramping, or split the rest of the way to allow rejointing, then the split will have to be filled. This can be done with wax filler or with wood. The advantage of wax filler is that it can be done quickly and without the need for sanding down or repolishing. Wax filler can be bought ready-made in various colours, or you can easily make your own (see Chapter 14). The filler is made warm by kneading in the hands and is pressed into the split with a piece of soft wood. The excess is then removed by rubbing over the surface with a waxy rag. The disadvantage of wax filler is that it becomes soft if warm and it can shrink in the cold. Therefore it is unsuitable for large or very open splits.

The advantage of wood is that it can be glued in place and so is permanent. It is possible to select wood with a matching grain, and the fact that it is glued in place helps to prevent the split getting any worse. The disadvantages of wood are that, after gluing, the wood will have to be planed and sanded flush with the surface and will have to be stained and polished to match the surrounding timber. It must be said that this type of repair is seldom successful on veneered tops that have a very decorative grain – it is almost impossible to match such grain, with the result that it has virtually to be painted on by putting colouring in the polish.

CHAPTER eight

Veneers

Three basic problems can arise with veneered surfaces: loose veneer on the edge, blisters or bubbles on the surface, and missing pieces of veneer.

LOOSE VENEER

This is probably the easiest of the problems to deal with. The veneer will have to be lifted very slightly and any dirt which has accumulated underneath cleaned out. For this purpose you will need a fine palette knife and a marquetry knife. Great care must be taken, because it is very easy to break the veneer when it is being lifted. It may be prudent to stick a strip of masking tape over the area first, to prevent any being lost if a piece does break off.

When it is clean under the veneer, new glue can be inserted underneath. You will find that a piece of stiff cardboard or the blade of a marquetry knife is ideal for this operation, being stiff enough to get the glue under the surface, but unlikely to damage the veneer in any way. You can use either hot animal glue or a modern woodworking adhesive, but if you choose the modern adhesive, more care must be taken when cleaning out underneath the veneer, as even the old glue will have to be removed. Press the veneer down firmly in place and squeeze out any excess glue, cleaning away with a damp cloth.

The veneer has now to be held in place while drying, and this can be done either with masking tape or by holding the veneer down with a block and G-cramp. It is a good idea, if you are holding it down with a

block, to place a few sheets of newspaper between the top surface of the veneer and the block so that any remaining excess glue will not cause it to stick.

BLISTERING

This occurs either because the glue underneath the veneer has perished or because insufficient glue was used when the veneer was originally laid; or it is possible that the veneer has been subjected to some damp on the surface, either by flood damage or by a flower vase or whatever being consistently placed on it. What is needed here also is new glue, but in order to get this new glue under the surface the blister has to be split with a marquetry knife in the direction of the grain. Again, if there is a danger of the veneer splitting badly, a strip of masking tape over the area will prevent pieces getting lost.

When the blister has been split in this way one side can be pressed down so that glue can be inserted under the other side. For this type of repair, hot glue is by far the best glue to use as it will be very difficult to clean out the old glue from under the veneer. When glue has been inserted under one side it can be pressed down very carefully and any excess glue squeezed out, and then glue inserted under the other half of the blister. It is very important at this stage to remove any excess glue by use of the veneer hammer. If the job is becoming cool then a little heat can be applied with an iron set to a medium temperature. Make sure, if you are using an iron, that you

82

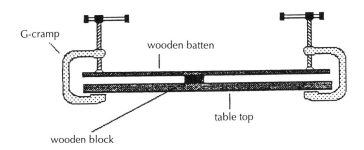

Fig. 79 Method for cramping down veneer which cannot be reached from the edge of the table.

have some glue spread on the top surface so the iron does not burn the veneer.

When all the excess glue has been removed the blister must be held down with a cramp. Again, place a few sheets of newspaper between the top surface and the block to prevent the block becoming stuck; it is important that the block should be quite warm, so as not to chill the glue. If it is not possible to reach the blister with a single G-cramp, then a long piece of wood or a batten must be placed over the block projecting to the sides of the work, where G-cramps can be fixed to both ends of the batten, which will in turn put pressure on the glue block. Always have hot water, an iron and a veneer hammer on hand when working with hot glue. It is no good going off to get them half-way through the job and allowing it to cool. Hot glue has to be used hot, and that means quickly, so have everything you will need on hand from the beginning.

MISSING PIECES

When repairing a top that has loose and missing veneer, always make sure all the loose veneer is stuck down before attempting to replace any of your missing pieces. Obviously the first step in replacement is to obtain some matching veneer. This does not mean just a similar grain,

although this is of course very important, but you must also have veneer of a similar thickness. You can use veneer that is slightly thicker than the original – indeed, this is sometimes preferable – but if your veneer is slightly thinner than the original then you will have to use a piece of brown paper underneath the veneer to make up the thickness, or in some extreme cases use two thicknesses of veneer. If you have access to a band saw, of course, you can cut your own veneer from a suitable piece of solid timber.

Now that you have your veneer, the next step is to decide what shape to make the replacement piece to be let in. As many joints as possible should be with the grain, diamond and triangle shapes being the most common, and it may be prudent, for example, to replace a slightly larger area than would at first seem necessary if this means that the joint or joints can be better concealed. When making a straight-sided joint the edge of the veneer can be planed carefully on a shooting block. However, on figured or burred veneer, straight sides should be avoided and fully curved pieces used; these pieces should always be as small as possible. Take a rubbing or tracing of the missing area of veneer and then cut a piece which will completely cover it and have all curved edges. Place your new piece of veneer over the missing area and mark around the edge with a fine scribe. You

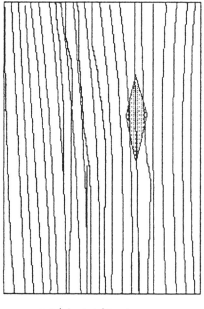
patch in straight grain

patch in curl grain

Fig. 80   Patching veneer.

now cut out the shape left by the scribe line. If you have a good selection of carving chisels you can cut the edges with an appropriately shaped chisel. If these chisels, however, are not available to you then you must use a marquetry knife. The new piece can then be glued and cramped in place and scraped level with the surface when dry. As it will be possible to clean the surface under the new piece of veneer, a modern cold glue can be used; this will avoid any undue expansion of the veneer.

VENEERING WITH SCOTCH GLUE

Hot (or scotch) glue is purchased in cake or pearl form and must be dissolved in water. It is best if the glue is left to soak for some time in cold water, before being heated in the inner glue pot. Just enough water to cover the glue in the pot should be used at first, more being added later as required. Keep the water as hot as possible in the outer pot, without allowing it to boil over, stirring the glue at regular intervals. When the glue is ready for use, a skin will form over its surface. The glue should then be tested for thickness. Pick up some of it on the glue brush and allow it to run back into the pot. It should run in a continuous stream, with no lumps or thick parts, and should not break into droplets. More water or glue can be added to get the required consistency.

When working with hot glue speed is of the essence, so everything that is likely to be needed should be prepared beforehand. All blocks etc. should be got ready and any cramps should be opened to the correct gap. A supply of hot water should be available and all the surfaces to be glued, all tools to be used and all blocks and presses etc. should be heated prior to use. The glue should not be brought in contact with any cold surface as this causes it to crystallize and the glue would not then be sufficiently adhesive.

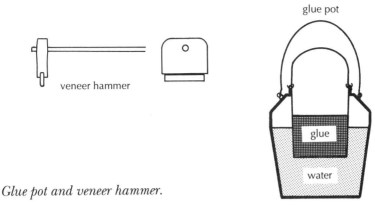

Fig. 81 Glue pot and veneer hammer.

HAMMER METHOD

The surface to be veneered should be made as flat as possible and then planed with a toothing plane. This is done both to increase the gluing area and to remove any high spots. After toothing, the groundwork should be treated with a size made of liquid glue mixed with water. Care must be taken to spread the size evenly over the surface; when it is dry, any high spots should be removed with the toothing plane. The veneer to be used should be made slightly damp with tepid water and then allowed to dry between two sheets of newspaper and kept flat between two flat pieces of wood with a weight on top. This will ensure that when you come to use the veneer it is quite flat.

When all has been prepared as described, a good layer of glue is spread onto the surface to be veneered and the veneer positioned in place. Glue is then spread on top of the veneer to act as a lubricant for the veneering hammer. Excess glue is squeezed out from under the veneer by pulling the veneering hammer over the surface at a slight angle to the grain, starting at the centre and working gradually towards the edge, squeezing out the glue as it goes. If the glue starts to harden and buckle the veneer, it can be

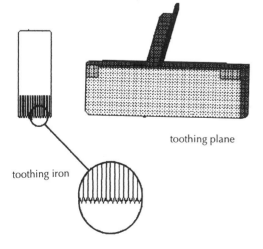

Fig. 82 A toothing plane.

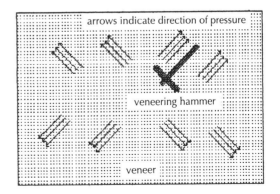

Fig. 83 Using the veneering hammer.

reheated with a warm iron. The surface of the veneer must be kept moist at all times by applying glue or size. When the veneer is in place, excess glue from the top of the veneer can be cleaned off with a hot, damp rag, but care must be taken not to get the surface too wet. Check the whole surface for areas that have failed to stick properly by tapping it with your finger. You will then be able to tell if it is solid or if the veneer has lifted. If the veneer is not secure a little more heat can be applied with an iron and the veneer hammered down again. If this fails to solve the problem, it may be necessary to split the veneer with a marquetry knife and insert more glue, hammering it down again, but this time work towards the cut just made and then cramp a caul or heated block over the area. Remember to put at least two sheets of newspaper under the block so that it can be more easily removed when dry.

If two or more pieces of veneer are to be jointed, such as with a quartered top, these are more successfully put down by the caul method (see below), but with care and experience it is possible to put them down with the hammer. Great care must be taken in positioning the veneer so that the joints are in the correct place and the grain matches: this is most important for a good end result. The veneers are allowed to overlap and a joint is cut with a chisel using a straight edge. The chisel is used to cut through both veneers where they overlap and the offcuts are carefully removed by gently lifting the veneer. It may be necessary to apply a little heat in order to lift the veneer without it splitting. The veneer around the joint is then put down with the hammer. When all the veneer is down, all joints between veneers should be covered with brown paper laid over the joint in the same way as the veneer. Rolls of gummed brown paper are available for just this purpose – if this is not done, it will be found that the joint will open up during drying. The veneered surface must now be left for

at least 24 hours to dry, then it can be cleaned up with the use of a cabinet scraper and medium to fine sandpaper. Remember that you are dealing with a very thin piece of wood – be careful not to go through the surface when cleaning up. Any veneer which overhangs the edge can be cleaned off with a file or sharp chisel, remembering always to file or cut away from the veneer. As these techniques require some practice, it would be a good idea to get some practice in putting down some odd pieces of veneer on some offcuts of wood before tackling an important job. It is an easy matter to break or split the veneer with the veneering hammer if there is too much glue under the veneer, or if the glue is too thick, or has not been hot enough.

If trouble is experienced and the glue starts to go off before the job is completed, then an ordinary household iron set to a medium temperature can be used to reheat the glue under the veneer. Be careful, however, not to have the iron too hot, and ensure that there is plenty of glue on top of the veneer when using the hot iron, to prevent burning.

CAUL METHOD

The caul method of laying veneer is the best method to use if several pieces of veneer are to be laid, or if the veneer is saw-cut and is too thick to be laid with a hammer. The groundwork is prepared in the same way as for hammer-laying. The caul itself is a sheet of timber or blockboard the size of the area to be veneered, and some cross-pieces to be cramped across the work. If more than one piece of veneer is being laid then the joints can be made beforehand and held in place with tape. Before applying any glue the caul and all blocks that are to be used, as well as the cramps themselves, should be heated, the caul itself being made quite hot. Glue

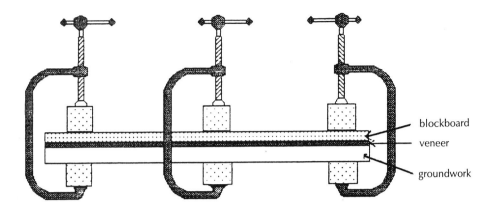

Fig. 84   Caul method of veneering.

is spread over the surface to be veneered and allowed to cool sufficiently not to expand the veneer on contact. In fact it is possible to allow the glue to become quite cold, although this is not necessary. The veneer is then laid carefully in place and held in position with a couple of veneer pins. The caul is now placed over the work and cramped in place. The heat from the caul will penetrate through the veneer and re-melt the glue. Pressure with the cramps should be applied working from the middle out, in order to squeeze out the excess glue.

APPLYING VENEER TO CURVED SURFACES

Veneers can be applied to curved surfaces, but must always be held with some form of cramp or other device until the glue is dry. It may be possible to accomplish this with a piece of masking tape, or by cutting a shaped block to hold the veneer in place. One method that is especially good when using hot glue is the sand bag. The sand is heated on a stove until quite hot and is then poured into a bag or sack, this heavy bag of sand then being used to keep the veneer in place until the glue is dry.

VENEERING WITH MODERN GLUE

When veneering relatively small areas of work, a good PVA glue such as Evo-Stick Woodworking is by far the easiest adhesive to use. The most important thing to remember is that any area of veneer stuck down must be held in place with a cramp until dry. Cross-banding and edging strips can often be held with a good-quality masking tape. If larger areas are to be veneered, the method is basically the same as the caul method for hot glue. It is vital that the ground is perfectly flat and that the entire area be covered with a block that is equally flat and of sufficient thickness to remain flat and not distort during cramping. It is no good simply applying G-cramps to the edges of this block — stout pieces of timber such as 3in by 2in (760mm × 500mm) must be cramped across the grain above and below the work. When applying the cramps, always make sure you tighten them evenly as you would the wheel-nuts of a car – each one a little at a time, starting as near as possible to the centre of the work and working outwards to expel the glue.

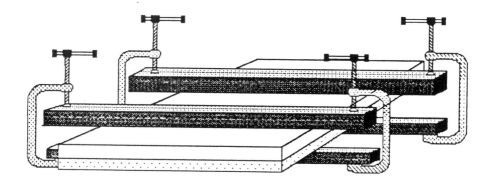

Fig. 85   Using modern glue.

MAKING A NEW TOP REUSING THE ORIGINAL VENEER

The first thing to do before any effort is made to remove the veneer is to make the new top and have it ready and prepared to accept the veneer. It should ideally be left a little bigger than the original, to allow for cleaning up after the veneer is laid. The big problem, of course, is to remove the old veneer without damaging it. First ensure that the veneer is in good repair and then cover the whole surface with masking tape. The tape should be laid strip by strip with no gaps and without overlapping. Next a piece of blockboard or MDF board slightly larger than the top should be glued onto the masking tape with a layer or two of newspaper between. The whole thing must be held flat in cramps until the glue is dry. When the glue has dried the original top can be cut away section by section, right down to the underside of the veneer. One good way of achieving this is with an electric router or planer. The underside of the veneer, which is now exposed and glued upside down on the blockboard, can be prepared gently with a toothing iron and then the new top glued onto it using the caul method of veneering. The whole thing must be held in the cramps overnight to dry. The only remaining task then is to remove the blockboard, but this should separate at the masking tape and newspaper without too much trouble by inserting a fine blade.

nine

Marquetry

Marquetry is the laying of veneers on a groundwork, these veneers being cut and shaped to make up a picture or pattern. If the pattern made is of a geometrical design, then this should more correctly be referred to as parquetry. The distinction between marquetry and inlay is that, in marquetry, both the pattern and the background are cut from veneers which are laid onto a solid ground. In inlay the pattern is inlaid directly into the solid ground.

ORIGINAL METHODS

Before I go into details of how to repair areas of damaged marquetry, I will give a brief outline of how marquetry panels were originally made. There are three kinds you may come across. The first, which is really inlay, is where a shape is cut out of one piece of veneer or solid timber and is inlaid into a solid background. The second type, a true marquetry, is where a pattern is cut out of two pieces of veneer at the same time. When the pattern has been cut out, the shape from one piece can easily be fitted into the offcuts of the other. It is of course possible to obtain two patterns in this way, one being the counterpart of the other. This was often done using tortoise-shell and brass and is called boulle and counterboulle, after the French cabinet-maker. The third type of marquetry is cut from many different pieces of veneer which are then fitted together to form a picture.

One of the biggest problems faced when making marquetry is, or rather was, how to obtain several very accurate copies of the pattern. These days, of course, it is possible to obtain as many as you want, just as long as you have access to a photocopier. In the past, before such miracles existed, a master pattern was drawn on a sheet of paper and all the lines of the pattern were pricked with a needle. The master pattern would then be placed over another sheet of paper and a fine bitumen powder would be applied from a pounce bag or 'dolly' made from coarse rag. The underlying paper would then be heated to near scorching point, which would secure the pounced pattern. As many copies as necessary could be produced in this way. Patterns produced in this manner were then stuck onto the veneers to be cut.

This procedure is carried out both on the shapes to be cut out and on the background veneer, and both pieces of marquetry are cut out with a marquetry saw. It is not possible to cut just one piece of veneer at a time without splitting it, so several layers should be cut at the same time, with waste wood on each side to take the 'rag' of the saw. The marquetry is then assembled and stuck down on paper. To lay the marquetry panel onto the ground, hot glue is applied to the ground wood, which has first been scored with a toothing plane. The hot glue is then allowed to cool and dry completely. When the glue has dried the panel is placed on the ground wood and is held in position with veneer pins. Next, a caul is made very hot and is held in position on top of the veneer with large wooden presses which have likewise been heated. It is important that everything – the ground wood, the layer of wood over the veneer and the presses themselves – is heated, so that when all is cramped in place securely, the heat penetrates through to the veneer and melts the glue. This elaborate process has to be used because if one attempted to lay a marquetry panel in the same way as ordinary veneer, expansion and distortion of the small pieces of veneer would make it virtually impossible, but with this process the veneer is held in place before the glue melts, and so distortion is kept to an absolute minimum.

One other process that may have to be done before the veneer is laid is to shade areas of light wood, to give the appearance of depth and roundness to flower petals and the like. This is achieved by dipping part of the piece of veneer into hot sand. Trial and error will tell you when the sand is at the right temperature. Hold a small piece of veneer in the sand with a pair of pliers or tweezers for five or six seconds – this should be long enough to give the desired effect. If the end of the veneer is too black and brittle after this length of time, then the sand is too hot.

REPLACING MISSING MARQUETRY

When we come to actually repairing areas of marquetry, of course, we hope it will not be necessary to replace entire panels, so it may be necessary to employ a different process and this will depend on the extent of the damage. The first thing to do in all cases is to stick down all the loose areas of veneer and allow them to dry. Then, if we are talking about a relatively small area of missing veneer, it may be possible to cut out and replace individual pieces. However, if a large area is missing, it may be necessary to make up a section and inlay this in one go. We will in any case have to make a pattern of the area that is missing. Sometimes it is possible to copy the pattern from somewhere else on the cabinet (a matching panel, for example). If this is not possible you will have to make a drawing of what you think is missing by examining carefully any other marquetry on the cabinet. Be sure, when you draw your pattern, that you draw it in the same manner as the rest of the marquetry on the cabinet. Do not try to make a better job than the original – the old and the new work must seem to have been done by the same hand.

If a single piece of marquetry is missing it will be possible to take a rubbing or trace the outline of the missing piece, stick the drawing onto a piece of veneer and cut it out. The advantage of sticking the drawing onto the veneer is that it helps to stop the veneer splitting, and it avoids compound error when having to transfer the drawing onto the veneer.

If several pieces are missing, make a drawing of the missing or damaged area, having first cleaned away any glue or dirt, and make several copies, depending on the number of different veneers involved. Select your veneer carefully for grain and thickness. On an item of eighteenth-century furniture the veneers will be quite thick, and if your supplier cannot provide veneer of the correct thickness in the wood you require, you may find it easier to cut your own. This is not as difficult as it may sound, with the aid of a good modern bandsaw. Set up a guide alongside the blade and slice the veneer from selected timber, a little thicker than actually required, to allow for cleaning up after the veneer is in place.

Having selected your veneer, stick your pattern on it, making sure the grain is in the right direction on the piece you intend to cut, and allow it to dry. You will then be ready to cut out the first piece of your pattern. When cutting veneer with a knife or scalpel it is important to have sharp tools and a good flat base for cutting on. If the work is very fine and there is a danger of losing a fine corner or intricate part, then it is a good idea to strengthen the veneer with gummed brown paper before cutting. Try the pieces together and carry out any small adjustments that may be required. Make sure that your assembled pieces fit into the original as a unit and make sure that all dirt and old glue have been cleaned away from the ground work. Decide how you are going to cramp your new work. Make sure you have all necessary blocks and cramps ready at hand before you apply any glue.

WINDOW METHOD

If a large area of marquetry is missing it is possible to make up the missing section as a unit and inlay the whole thing in one go. The window method is a good way of making up a section of marquetry, both for replacing an area of a large panel and for making up small motifs such as shells or sunbursts.

The picture is drawn on a light-coloured piece of waste veneer. One part of the picture is then cut out, using a very sharp marquetry knife. Do not try to cut through the veneer in one go – use the point of the knife in a series of short pricking cuts, rather than a long sweep. It may be necessary to go over the line several times in this manner before the veneer comes away. Once the piece has been cut out of the waste veneer, a window has been created and the veneer to be used can be placed behind it. Hold the veneer in place with tape behind the window, and cut the veneer using the edges of the window as a guide. Only cut part of the way through at this stage. Once the veneer is marked in this way the tape can be removed and the veneer placed on a suitable board for final cutting. If a very large or complicated picture is being made, with small pieces

Fig. 86 The window method for cutting marquetry.

(a) picture drawn on a piece of light-coloured waste veneer.

(b) one section cut out to form a window.

*(c)   window placed over veneer to be cut to act
as a template.*

(d)   veneer cut ready to be inserted into window.

(e)   next section cut out to form a window.

(g)   next section cut out.

(f)   placed over veneer to be cut.

(h)   finished picture.

being inlaid in larger ones, it may be a good idea to do all the larger pieces first and then overlay this picture with a drawing of the smaller bits and repeat the process. When the picture is complete it can be let into the original marquetry.

LIFTING MARQUETRY

It may be that, although your marquetry is damaged and lifting, no pieces are actually missing. In this case, of course, what is needed is to get some fresh glue under the veneer and cramp it down. If the damage is fairly recent it may be possible to simply lift one corner of a piece of inlay, inject some glue under and cramp it down again. Make sure when you do this that you squeeze all the excess glue back out before you cramp it, or you will end up with a bump in your marquetry. If, however, the damage is old, it is possible that dirt has accumulated under the veneer. This will have to be removed before gluing, otherwise the dirt will cause a bump and will probably stop the glue from sticking effectively. It may be possible to accomplish this by just lifting part of the veneer and cleaning underneath, but it may be necessary to remove part of the pattern. The part you choose to remove should come away easily – it will only be held at the edges – but nevertheless, care must be taken not to break it. All dirt and old glue must be thoroughly cleaned away from the ground and from the back of the veneer before regluing. It is possible, especially if the damage was caused by water, that the veneer in question will be warped and enlarged. Before gluing, try the pieces in place dry to ensure they fit, and adjust with a marquetry knife if necessary. If any of the pieces are warped it may be necessary to dampen them and allow them to dry between sheets of newspaper with a weight on them, so that they are flat before replacing. Remember to squeeze out all excess glue and place newspaper under any block to make sure it does not stick to the work.

A VERY TRICKY PROBLEM

One other problem that you may come up against, usually the result of woodworm, is when the veneer itself is in good condition, but the construction wood underneath is damaged. Three courses of action are possible. Firstly, it may be possible, if you have access from the reverse side, to cut away the damaged section of wood under the veneer and replace it without touching the veneer itself. If this means of repair is undertaken a piece of wood should be cramped over the face of the veneer during the repair to give it support. Secondly, it may be necessary to lift an area of veneer by the use of a hot iron and a wet rag, carry out the repair and then relay the veneer. Thirdly and most drastically, it may be necessary to remove the entire area of veneer, replace the top or panel and relay the original veneer.

LIFTING VENEER

If it is necessary to lift a piece of veneer so that a repair can be undertaken, you will need a supply of hot water, some rags and an iron. Have ready some sheets of timber and weights, so that the veneer can be placed on a flat bed between sheets of newspaper and weighted down until dry.

To lift the veneer, place a hot, wet rag over the area to be lifted and apply heat with a hot iron. Continue to do this until the veneer shows signs of lifting, at which time you should assist the lifting with the aid of a pallet knife or wallpaper scrape. Be very careful not to damage the veneer with the tools. Be patient, and allow the hot water to work using the knife or scrape. As you work your way along the veneer, put pieces of wood under the parts already lifted to prevent them re-adhering. As soon as the veneer is free, wash and scrape off the remains of glue from the reverse side of the veneer. Dab dry with a dry cloth and place under the weights on a flat bed between sheets of newspaper, so that the veneer will dry flat for regluing.

ten

Polishing

Most very early furniture was painted, but during the sixteenth century this practice declined and more and more furniture was simply oiled or waxed. Nut or linseed oil was used, which had the effect of darkening the wood. Wax, on the other hand, imparted a honey tone. Both methods were used with many variations until the introduction of French polishing around 1820. Cabinet-makers would have had their own formula, using oil, turpentine and beeswax, brick dust, copal varnish and red lead in varying proportions.

Before deciding to strip and repolish a piece of antique furniture it must first be ascertained whether or not the old polish can be saved. Washing with hot soapy water and very fine wire wool, then waxing, can have remarkable results. Remember that the old polish and patina on a piece of furniture are the things that make it what it is and that give it its market value, and should only be removed as a last resort.

French polishing is by far the most difficult finish to achieve and is a trade in itself. A great deal of experience is needed before one can obtain professional results. A wax finish, on the other hand, can be achieved relatively easily.

REMOVING OLD POLISH

Whichever finish you decide is most appropriate, you will of course have to remove the old polish first and this can be quite easily and safely done with a proprietary paint remover such as Nitromors. Do *not* scrape the old polish off, as this can alter the colour and patina of the piece of furniture irretrievably. Avoid caustic soda at all costs. It is not only dangerous and unpleasant to use but is very harmful to furniture.

Nitromors paint remover will not harm the wood in any way, but some precautions will have to be taken to prevent its damaging the user. Stripper should only be used in a well-ventilated area, as the fumes can be harmful, and contact with the skin is definitely to be discouraged. It is also worth remembering that stripper will eat its way into rubber and plastic, so ordinary household gloves are no protection and plastic spectacles and watch faces are at its mercy. Also keep electric cables well clear as the stripper can eat through the insulation. I recommend the wearing of safety goggles and stout gardening gloves when stripping furniture.

Brush the paint remover onto the surface to be stripped, using an old paintbrush, wait a short time for it to start working, then take it off very carefully with a fine steel wool, preferably 0000 grade. If there is a great deal of polish on the surface then a coarser wool such as grade 1 can be used. Be careful not to rub too hard with the steel wool – remember that it is the paint remover that removes the old polish. The steel wool is used to remove the paint remover – never be tempted to rub a little harder if the polish is almost off but the stripper is nearly dry. Apply more stripper and give it time to work. Care and patience will pay dividends with the end result.

Once the old polish has been removed completely (it is essential to ensure that the last trace of polish is gone), it will be necessary to wash the whole surface with methylated spirit to ensure all trace of stripper has been removed.

Next on the agenda is the colour of the piece of furniture, and here a difficult question arises. All furniture fades over the years, so the question is do we apply stain and colour it back to what we think it would have been like originally, or do we apply no colour at all and have it exactly as it comes? Surely we should do only what is necessary to preserve the piece of furniture and not go messing about with the colour that the natural processes of time have given it? Well I think we can be justified in making a compromise. For instance, if a piece has been unpleasantly bleached by strong sunlight, then I feel we are justified in restoring some of its original warmth and colour, but if the piece has faded over the years to a nice mellow, pleasing colour, then why not leave well alone?

STAINING

If the decision is taken to alter the colour, how do we do it? It is difficult to explain what to do because each case is different and will require different treatment. Let us keep it simple and say that if you want to alter the colour substantially, then this is best done with either a water stain or a naphtha stain, the water stain being by far the cheapest.

Naphtha stain is purchased ready to use and is the type of stain you are likely to get from a DIY shop. It is very good for some jobs, but do be careful because the effects can be very dramatic. The advantage of naphtha stains is that they will not raise the grain of the wood, as water stains are inclined to do on new timber, but it is not possible to wax directly on top of them as the turpentine in the wax will act as a solvent

and might remove the stain. Consequently this type of stain should only be used under shellac.

Water stains are bought as a powder or crystals and have to be added to hot water and then allowed to cool. Because you mix the stain yourself you have a far greater control over the eventual colour, as it is of course possible to mix oak, walnut or mahogany stain together to obtain the desired result. Always try out your stain, either on a separate piece of wood or somewhere underneath the cabinet that doesn't show, to make sure that it is the correct colour and not too dark. One disadvantage of water stain is that it tends to raise the grain of the wood. Although this will not be a problem on old, polished surfaces that have only been stripped, it will cause a problem with new or resurfaced timber. This problem is overcome by applying hot water to the surface before staining, in order to raise the grain. The water applied should be dried with the aid of a hair dryer on medium heat. It is important not to allow the water to become cold on the surface, as this can cause a black stain to appear, especially on oak. This process may have to be repeated more than once, until the surface no longer feels rough when the hot water has dried. At this stage the water stain can be applied with little risk of it raising the grain of the wood.

The water stain is wiped onto the surface to be coloured with a cloth or fine steel wool and any excess is wiped off with a pad or soft cloth. The use of wire wool when applying the stain is necessary on occasions, because after stripping and washing with methylated spirit the surface can be difficult to penetrate. The stain must be wiped off in the direction of the grain and you must be meticulous not to leave any marks or streaks in the wet stain – these are impossible to remove when dry except by washing the whole lot off and starting again. Do one part of the cabinet at a time and do not allow the water stain to dry before being wiped off. When the stain is dry, application of a little clean methylated spirit will show you what the colour will be like when the polish is applied. If you still want to alter the colour slightly then a small quantity of dry colouring pigments, obtainable from polishing manufacturers, can be put into the polish itself, but remember that anything put in the polish will to some extent cover the grain, so use these dry colours sparingly. Assuming that the piece of furniture is now the desired colour, we can apply polish.

WAX POLISHING

If we have decided on a wax finish then we first have to make up some wax. Shred some beeswax into a bowl with some turpentine. Place the bowl in a saucepan of hot water and stir until the beeswax has dissolved, colour with some dry colouring pigment as required – perhaps some mineral black and Venetian red – and then add a little copal varnish to harden it when it cools. Do not have the wax so hard that it is difficult to apply; better to have it soft and leave it to stand for a few hours before buffing up. It will be necessary to repeat the operation several times to obtain a good result, which will involve a great deal of elbow grease.

A QUICK METHOD

Alternatively you could apply two or three coats of shellac with a polishing mop. This must be done with the grain and allowed to dry for about half an hour before being rubbed down with either fine steel wool or flour paper, and another coat of polish applied. After the last coat has dried it must again be rubbed down lightly and then waxed. The application of a couple of coats of shellac before waxing means that much of the grain will be filled and less wax and

less hard work will be needed. There are many preparatory waxes on the market which can be obtained from polish manufacturers and even some antique dealers. Make sure they have a beeswax base and are free of silicon.

FRENCH POLISHING

French polishing is a process by which a very high gloss can be obtained. It is most suitable for furniture which is inlaid with marquetry and, of course, grand pianos, which are traditionally French polished. The polish is applied with a pad, or rubber, which is a wad of cotton wool covered with a clean cotton rag. To make a pad, take some cotton wool and shape it to fit in the hand comfortably with the fingers wrapped around the sides. How large a piece will depend on the size of the job. Place the shaped cotton wool inside a stocking leg and tie it off. This will help it to keep its shape and prevent bits of wool escaping and getting onto the work. Cover the whole thing in a piece of clean, washed cotton rag. Always remove the rag when recharging the pad with polish.

The process of French polishing can be divided into three stages. The first stage is where the polish is fairly thick and the idea is to get as much as possible onto the job. This process is known as fadding and on new timber would be done with a fad, which is a rubber with only a very coarse cover. However, on antique work which has been stripped this stage can largely be skipped and a proper rubber used from the outset, with the shellac diluted 40 per cent with methylated spirit. The second stage is where there is plenty of polish on the job and the polish in the pad is quite thin. The idea is to work the polish and get it into the grain of the wood. The pad is rubbed continually over the surface in figure-of-eight movements, applying a small amount of polish at a time and also burnishing the surface. Remember to concentrate on covering the edges and getting into the corners, and remember that at no time should the pad be stationary on the work. The third stage comes when the grain is completely filled and is called 'spiriting off'. Make a completely new pad and, instead of filling it with polish, put just a few drops of methylated spirit onto the cotton wool and cover with a clean rag, then place the pad into an airtight container until the spirit has permeated right through the pad. The pad is then used in the same way as before and this will gradually remove the oil from the surface and impart that extra little shine. If, when you rub a finger over the surface of the job, it leaves a trace, then you know that there is still some oil on the surface. When all of the oil is gone, then you know that your job is complete.

Do not expect to obtain a perfect result first time. Remember, the pad must be moving at all times and never be stationary on the work. Remember to concentrate on the edges and corners; the centre of the work will take care of itself. And remember that only practice will tell you how much pressure is needed on the pad at any given time.

To start, the pad is filled with polish which has been thinned with meths to about two parts polish to three parts methylated spirits. It should be filled so that, when it is squeezed lightly, polish oozes through the cotton rag. The pad is then wiped over the surface to be polished, first in the direction of the grain, leaving a thin film of polish behind. At first, when the pad is very wet, a lot of polish will be squeezed out and care must be taken not to go over the same area twice until the polish is seen to dry, but gradually as the pad dries you will find that you can go back over an area almost at once without the pad sticking. This is when you must go over the job in as many directions as possible, using circular and figure-of-eight movements; keep working in this way until the pad is dry. The pad can be refilled several times – the idea at this stage is to get as much polish as possible onto the surface without the pad sticking. The polish must now be left overnight to harden and then it can be rubbed down with flour paper or fine steel wool and the process repeated, but this time with slightly more dilute polish. The pad can then be kept in an airtight container when not in use.

This process must be continued until the grain of the wood is filled completely. You will find that the grain in the middle of your job will fill more quickly than at the edges and corners, so it is a good idea to try and concentrate your efforts on the outside edges and make sure you get right into those corners. The biggest danger you will encounter when polishing in this way is 'burning' the polish. This is where you go over an area before the polish has had a chance to dry. This is usually because you have put the pad down a little hard on the job and too much polish has come out, consequently taking longer to dry. When you go over this wet area of polish, instead of leaving more polish on a job, you are more likely to take off that which is already there. When this happens you must not try to build it up again right away, which will only result in failure with even more polish being removed. You must leave the job overnight until it can be rubbed down. The other thing that can cause burning is polish getting sticky on the edge of your pad, so always make sure that you have a clean pad. If the pad feels at all sticky, change to a clean area of rag. It is possible to make life a little easier when polishing by lubricating the surface with a little polishing oil. This is used by smearing a small amount onto the palm of the hand and then wiping the edge of the pad in it. Use the oil sparingly, because it leaves a film on the job which has to be removed later. As you gain more experience with polishing you will use less oil.

After the work has been left overnight, it can be rubbed down with fine flower paper or 0000 wire wool and the process repeated. As the work progresses, use ever more dilute polish, ending up with polish which is more spirit than shellac.

OIL FINISHING

Even after the introduction of French polishing, oil finishes were still used for some work. Dining table tops in particular benefited from oil finishing, as it gave a far more heat-resistant finish than French polish.

As with wax, there are several recipes for oil finishes, one of which is one part cold-drawn linseed oil simmered for ten minutes and then strained through a cotton rag. One-eighth turpentine is then added and thoroughly mixed over a low heat.

The oil is applied daily over the course of five or six weeks, being well rubbed into the timber and any excess wiped off. Before the next application of oil the surface is washed with cold water, to remove any dirt or dust.

eleven

Cramping

TYPES OF CRAMP

Any joint which has been glued, with the possible exception of the dovetail joint, needs to be held in place for the time it takes the glue to dry. Sometimes, when a small piece of wood needs to be held in place, this can be accomplished with masking tape, but mostly a cramp or spring will be needed. Listed below are the most common types of cramps and their uses.

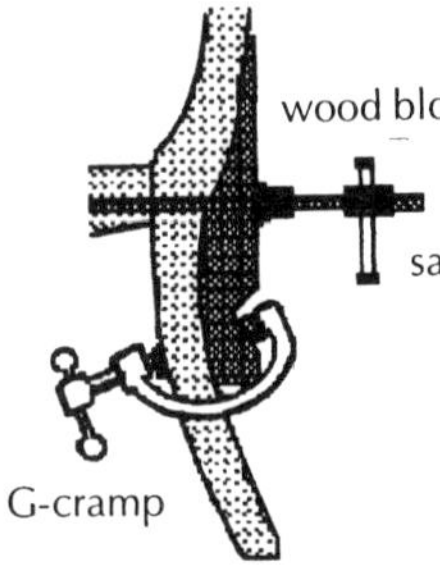

SASH CRAMP

The sash cramp is possibly the most useful cramp, as it can be used for gluing together a great variety of pieces of furniture, tables, cabinets and most chair joints. Always remember to put a wooden block between the wood of the cabinet and the cramp – otherwise, when the pressure is applied the cramp can easily cause damage. *Never* over-tighten a cramp. Once the joint is home and the shoulders of, say, a mortise and tenon joint are touching, then only sufficient pressure to hold the joint in place is required. I have seen people continuing to tighten a cramp when a joint was not quite home, even though the cramp itself was bending and it was quite obvious there was an obstruction stopping the joint going together properly.

Sometimes the shape of the piece of furniture being glued does not easily lend itself to being cramped; this is often the case with chairs. When this occurs it is necessary to cut a shaped block to accom-

Fig. 87   Wooden block cut to accommodate sash cramp and held in place with a G-cramp.

modate the cramp. This has to be done for two reasons: first, to prevent the cramp from slipping out of place and secondly, to ensure that the line of pressure from the cramp is in line with the joint. It is important to remember when using any cramp that the line of force must always be in line with the joint, otherwise distortion can occur. Always check when you have finished cramping that the cabinet or piece of furniture which you are cramping together is square and that the cramps have not pulled it out of shape. This is especially important in the case of chairs.

G-CRAMP

The G-cramp is useful for a whole range of jobs, including splices and holding the shaped blocks needed for cramping shaped work. The G-cramp can also be used to hold down areas of veneer. It is also useful for holding pieces in place whilst they are being screwed together.

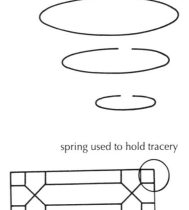

spring used to hold tracery

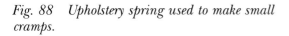

cut each coil to obtain the springs

Fig. 88   Upholstery spring used to make small cramps.

UPHOLSTERY SPRINGS

Upholstery springs can be cut to use as small G-cramps. They are especially useful when repairing delicate items, such as fretwork or carving.

WEBBING CRAMPS

Webbing cramps are strips of webbing with

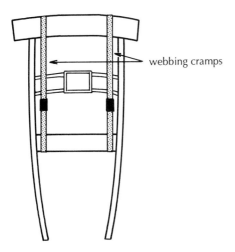

webbing cramps

Fig. 89   Webbing cramps.

a ratchet attachment at one end, which can be wrapped around a job and then tightened with a screwdriver. They are very useful on shaped work and can be used to hold down the headrails on chairs.

CRAMPING CHAIRS

Chairs are by far the most difficult of items to cramp, as they hardly ever have a square line to them. Remember that there are two types that need to be cramped: the side-assembled and the back-assembled.

SIDE-ASSEMBLED

Glue the various pieces of the sides together and allow to dry before assembling the rest of the chair. It will be necessary with this type of chair to cut shaped blocks to protect the chair from being bruised by the cramps, and to stop the cramps slipping.

When the chair is cramped up there are two very important things to check: first that the seat frame is flat – this can be done by sighting along the top of two seat rails of

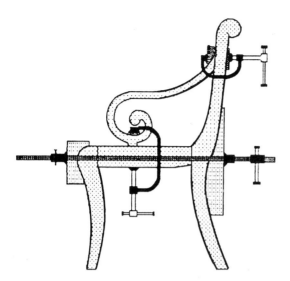

Fig. 90   Use of shaped blocks when cramping a chair.

the chair to make sure that they are parallel. If they are not, it may be necessary to alter the line of the cramps very slightly. Experiment by moving one cramp slightly to see whether that helps or makes the fault worse. If necessary, tip the cramp in the other direction and re-tighten. Don't worry unduly about whether the chair rocks on the floor – the length of the leg can be altered to adjust that, but once the glue is dry it is impossible to alter the angle of the seat. The second thing to check is that the seat is square, and this is done by measuring from corner to corner. The distance from a to b in Fig. 92 should be the same, or at least nearly the same, as from c to d.

BACK-ASSEMBLED

With a back-assembled chair it is the various parts of the back, and the front legs and front seat rail, that have to be glued up

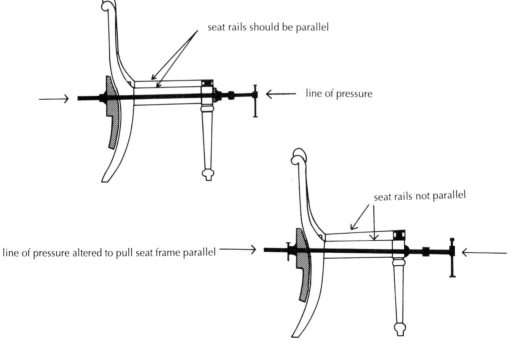

seat rails should be parallel

line of pressure

seat rails not parallel

line of pressure altered to pull seat frame parallel

Fig. 91   Adjusting position of cramps so that seat frame is flat.

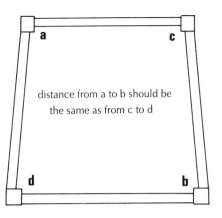

Fig. 92   Checking that the seat is square.

give a hard and fast rule for cramping – sometimes a webbing cramp will do the job, sometimes it will take a sash cramp with a specially cut block.

SHAPED SEATS

Chairs with shaped seats will need special blocks cut to accommodate the cramps, and these blocks will have to be held in place with G-cramps. Remember, as always, that the line of pressure must be in line with the joint. That is to say that, if a line could be drawn between the two points of contact at each end of the cramp, this line should pass through the middle of the joint. It is a good idea with this type of chair to cramp together the front leg assembly and allow this to dry first, and then cramp the rest of the seat frame and the front legs together in one operation. However, if for one reason or another this is not possible, maybe because there is not enough room

and allowed to dry. Once these two assemblies are dry they can be united by the side seat rails and any understretchers. Arms are best fitted at this time as well. (See Chapter 4.)

The headrails of chairs come in all shapes and sizes and it is not possible to

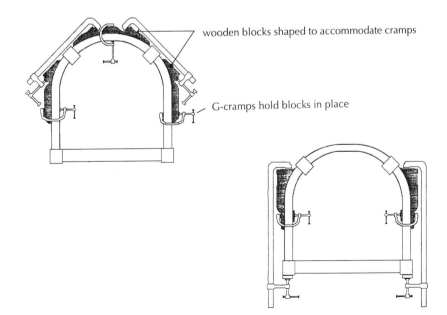

Fig. 93   Gluing the rear legs on a shaped seat.

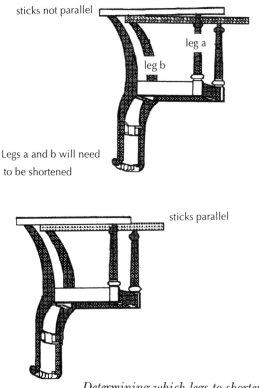

sticks not parallel

leg a

leg b

Legs a and b will need
to be shortened

sticks parallel

Determining which legs to shorten.

for all the necessary blocks, then the seat frame *apart* from the front legs should be glued together. If this is done, the front legs should be put in place but not glued or cramped. By doing this you are not dealing with too many blocks, but you are sure that the ends of the side seat rails are the correct distance apart where they join the front legs.

If, when a chair has been glued together, the seat frame is square and level, but it is found that the chair rocks when placed on a level surface, then one of the legs will have to be cut. The way to determine which leg is to be cut is to turn the chair upside down on a bench and place two parallel pieces of wood across the legs – either one across the back two legs and one across the front two, or one across the left-hand legs and one across the right-hand legs – and then sight across these two pieces of wood

to see if they are parallel. If they are not, then the appropriate leg will have to be cut to make them parallel.

OTHER USES
AREAS THAT CANNOT BE REACHED

If the area to be cramped is in the middle of a table top and cannot be reached with a single cramp, then the following method can be used. Place a solid block of wood over the area to be glued (remembering to place paper between this block and the area being glued, to prevent any excess glue from sticking to the block itself), then place a batten or other long piece of wood across the block and cramp each end. This will apply pressure to the block in the area where the pressure is required. Care must be taken to support the work and prevent the top or panel from splitting when using this method of cramping – the easiest way to achieve this will probably be to cramp a batten above and below the work first to give it support.

CRAMPING INSIDE A CABINET

On occasions it may be necessary to cramp inside a cabinet, for instance when gluing in a new drawer guide or runner. On these occasions it may be possible to spring a piece of wood or a dowel rod across between the piece being glued and the opposite side of the chest.

CRAMPING A HALF-ROUND OR D-END TABLE TOP

When cramping a half-round or D-end table top, you will have to cut pieces of wood to fit the shape of the top. It will also be necessary to cramp battens across the top, both above and below. This has to be done to ensure that the top does not fold up under the pressure of the cramps. The battens are also a good way of ensuring that the top surfaces remain flush. If, when the top is glued up, the top surface is not flush, then wedges can be inserted under the battens in the appropriate place, and tapped in with a hammer until the top is flush. Care must be taken to tighten the sash cramps evenly, or there may be a tendency for the top to slip, especially if the joint in the top is not straight across.

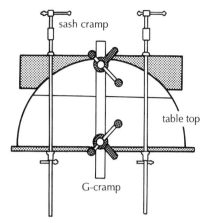

batten top and bottom to keep top flat

Fig. 95   Method of cramping a half-round table top.

105

twelve

Glass

REPLACING DOOR PANES

When a pane of glass gets broken in a glazed door, examine the glass carefully to see if it is modern or old glass. If it is antique, blown glass, it will have ridges and imperfections in it, and unless it is badly broken it may not be desirable to replace it. If it is modern glass, or if it has to be replaced because it is badly damaged, the first job to be tackled is to remove the jagged remains of the pane. This is not always an easy matter, especially if it's a tracery door. On some doors the glass may be held in place with a bead. If this is the case it will be a relatively easy matter to prise the beading off with a palette-knife or chisel, but be careful not to damage the surrounding wood. One way of protecting the edge is to hold a thin piece of metal, like the blade of a wall-paper scrape, against the edge and use a palette-knife or screwdriver against this to prise off the bead. Always do any prising away as close to a pin as possible. Be careful not to break the bead – prise it away a little and this may lift the head of the pins securing it just enough to get hold of them with a pair of pinchers. If the heads of the pins pull through the bead rather than being lifted by it, then they will have to be removed after the bead.

Your problems really begin if the pane you are replacing is in a tracery door. In this case you will be dealing with very delicate glazing bars and the glass will most probably be held in with putty. You may be tempted to work with the door lying flat, so that the bars have some support, and there is some merit in this; however, you have to be meticulous in removing the bits of glass and putty before they have a chance to get underneath the door and scratch the polish. Personally I prefer to work with the door in an upright position so that all the bits fall straight to the floor where they can do no harm.

Heat will have to be applied to the putty to soften it, and this is best achieved with the use of a soldering iron. Hold the hot soldering iron against the putty until it starts to soften and follow behind with an old chisel. At several points around the pane it will be held with a small pin, or more often than not a small triangular piece of zinc which has been pressed into the glazing bar. These pins or pieces of zinc can be removed with a pair of pliers or pinchers, and then any remaining putty and fragments of glass can be removed. It is especially important to make sure that no hard fragment remains on the underside of the astragal moulding, as this could break the new piece of glass when it is being bedded in.

CUTTING GLASS

STRAIGHT GLASS

Cutting straight-sided glass is very easy, and all that is really needed is confidence. Make sure the glass is clean before attempting to cut it, and have it resting on a clean, flat surface. *Always wear safety glasses when cutting glass.* Use a wooden straight-edge to

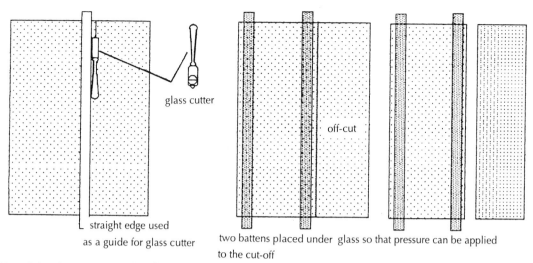

Fig. 96   Cutting straight glass.

run your glass-cutter along and make sure your cutter is sharp. Run the glass-cutter across the glass in a single sweep with a constant firm pressure, making sure that you start the cut right at the very edge and continue to cut until the cutter runs off the other edge. When the cut is complete, place a thin batten underneath the glass, with one edge directly under the cut. If it is a large piece of glass place another batten underneath so that the piece you want is lying flat. Apply even pressure along the length of the unsupported offcut and it should break away clean. On thicker glass it is sometimes necessary to tap with a small hammer underneath the cut to make sure that the cut is deep enough, but be very careful if you do this because small slivers of glass may fly up, so watch out for your eyes and be careful not to get glass splinters in your hands when handling the glass afterwards.

SHAPED GLASS

Most glass retailers will be glad to cut a piece of shaped glass for you. You can either take the door to them, or you can cut

a cardboard template of the missing pane for them. If you choose to make a template, ensure that it is not too tight a fit, but also be sure that the edge is covered by the moulding all the way around and does not show from the outside of the door when fitted.

If the piece of glass you are replacing was antique, it may be worth having a look around the local auctions, where you may find some old prints or paintings going cheap. It is possible that these prints, although of no great value in themselves, will have old or antique glass in the frames.

If you choose to cut the curved glass yourself, you will first need to mark out the piece you want on the glass. Make a cardboard template of the piece you want, and place this on the glass. You can now either mark around your template with a felt-tip pen, or you can dab putty around the edge, half over the template and half over the glass, which will leave an impression of the shape you want when the template is removed. If you choose to use felt-tip pen, remember that the shape you draw will be bigger than the original and that you will have to cut on the inside of the line. Decide which edge to cut first – you don't want to

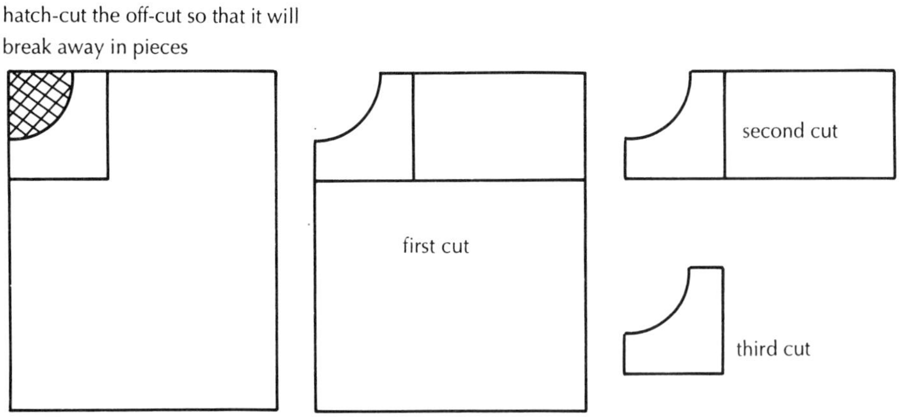

hatch-cut the off-cut so that it will
break away in pieces

first cut

second cut

third cut

Fig. 97   Cutting shaped glass.

end up with a curved cut that leaves you with a point or acute angle. Normally I would say that it is best to cut the curved edge or edges first, in which case you will have to position the template so that the curve is near a corner and not facing the centre of your glass, as this would be wasteful in terms of the amount of glass used. If your curve is only slight it may be possible to treat it in much the same way as a straight cut, supporting the main piece and applying pressure to the offcut. However, if the curve is not so slight it is often a good idea to make a few cuts in

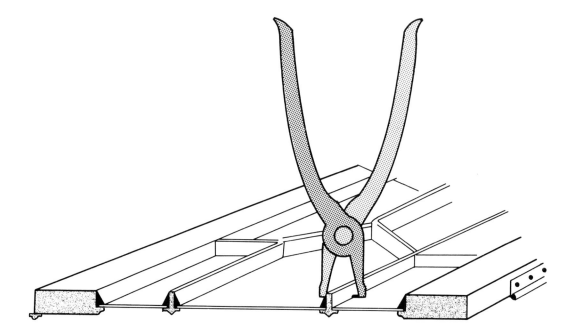

Fig. 98   Using pliers to squeeze in pins on a glazing bar.

different directions on the waste piece so that it can be removed piecemeal.

When the new piece of glass is ready, ensure that the glazing bars are clean and bed the new glass in on soft putty. It is possible to obtain wood casement putty in a dark colour for use with hardwood windows; it is also possible to alter the colour of putty by adding some of the dry earth colours. It is important that the putty is soft and lump free, otherwise it is easy to break the glass when bedding in. Once the glass is bedded in, small pins or triangles of zinc will need to be tapped into the glazing bars to secure the glass in place; the putty alone will not be enough. Tapping the pins into the glazing bars is a very delicate operation and on the more delicate bars it is better to squeeze them in with a pair of pliers. Once the pins are in place and the glass secure, the glass can then be puttied in around the edge and the excess cleaned away with a putty knife. If, when the putty is fully dry (this may take several days), it is still not the correct colour, it can be adjusted by polishing over it with button polish which has had some dry colours added to it.

thirteen

Keys and Locks

Basically there are two types of lock that you will come up against: the ward lock and the lever lock. These two types of lock will be found in many guises, such as door locks, drawer locks and box locks, of both mortise and surface fittings.

The idea of any lock is simple: a key is inserted into the lock over a pin which allows the key to rotate. In rotating, the key comes into contact with a locking bar, which is moved forwards or backwards depending on which way the key is turned. A lock that has no more than that will work, but it will not be secure because almost any key of the correct length will open it. To make the lock secure, obstacles or 'wards'

are riveted to the backplate of the lock. In this way only a key which has been cut in such a way as to avoid these wards will turn.

Another method of making the lock secure, rather than having the key avoid wards, is to make it so that levers have to be moved into a certain position by the key to allow the locking bar to move. Lever locks are an improvement on ward locks because wards are easy to bypass with the use of a skeleton key. (A skeleton key is simply a key which has had most of the body of the key removed so that it avoids any wards when it is rotated in the lock.)

flush-fitting door lock

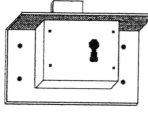

flush-fitting drawer lock

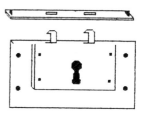

flush-fitting box lock

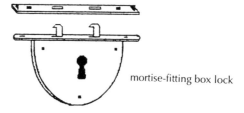

mortise-fitting box lock

Fig. 99   Four types of lock.

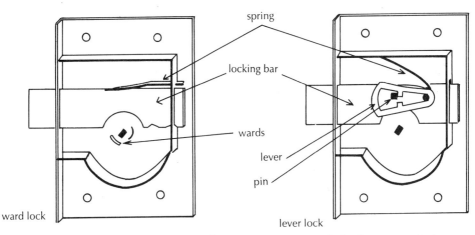

Fig. 100   A ward lock and a lever lock.

MAKING A KEY

To make a key, it will be best to take the lock apart. Sometimes the backplate of the lock is screwed to the faceplate and sometimes it is riveted through. If the backplate is riveted it will be necessary to file off the burr from the back of the rivets and prise off the plate. Once the plate has been removed it will be easy to see what shape the key needs to be to rotate and move the locking bar. It is best if you can obtain a selection of old keys and adjust one of these to fit the lock; however, if these are not available, blank keys can be purchased from most locksmiths. One of the big drawbacks to using new key blanks is that the bows of the keys tend to be rather ugly and not at all in keeping with a piece of antique furniture, although it is possible to cut the bow of an old key and solder it onto the end of your key blank; alternatively, some suppliers of reproduction locks and handles also sell decorative key bows.

To change the bow of a key, simply cut off the old bow and file down the end of the key shank so that you have a small dowel on the end, drill the bow to accept this dowel and solder it in place.

OPENING LOCKS WITHOUT THE KEY

Once in a while a key will be lost when the door or drawer is locked. If it is not possible to obtain access by removing the back or top of the cabinet or by any other means, it may be necessary to make a key without taking the lock apart. This can be done with a ward lock. First, it is worth trying any old ward key that you can get hold of – you may be lucky enough to find one that works. If you cannot find an old key that works, obtain a blank that can just be inserted into the keyhole. Next file down the depth of the key so that it will begin to rotate in the lock. Now you have a key which is the right size, and all you have to do is to file it so that it avoids the wards. If you light a candle and hold the end of the key in the flame it will become black with soot. Now carefully insert the blackened key into the lock and rotate it as far as it will go. When you remove the key you will be able to see where it touched the wards, and it can be filed appropriately.

With a lever lock, things are not quite so simple. The first thing to try is to insert a fine blade between the door and the door

111

stile, up against the locking-bar. Exert pressure on the locking-bar with the blade, trying to push it back away from the door stile. At the same time as you are exerting pressure on the bar, insert a piece of stiff bent wire, such as a hairpin, into the lock and try to move the levers. It is just possible that the bar will move if you get the levers in the right position. If this course of action is unsuccessful, very carefully lever the door away from the door stile, using a screwdriver, taking care not to bruise either the door or the stile, by using a wallpaper or cabinet scrape on either side of the screwdriver. It is often found on old cabinets that shrinkage has left a larger gap than intended between door and stile, so that the locking-bar only just catches and the door will not have to be prised far for it to open. The lock can then be removed and a key made in the manner described previously.

If it is not possible to get inside the cabinet by removing the back, the door cannot be prised open and the lock cannot be picked, it would seem that you have no alternative but to actually cut the locking-bar, or carefully cut away a section of the door stile, just big enough for the bar to pass. Cutting the bar is the very last resort, especially if you are dealing with an unusual or rare lock. Great care must be taken to cause as little damage as possible. Prise the door and door stile apart sufficiently to be able to insert a hacksaw blade. I have found that sticking two or three strips of masking tape on either side will help to prevent the blade doing too much damage.

NON-CATCHING LOCKS

Sometimes it will be found that, although the lock operates, the locking bar no longer reaches far enough across to catch in the stile. In this case, if we are talking about a later brass lock, it may be possible to take it apart and solder an extra piece of brass onto the end of the locking-bar, to extend it. With an iron lock it will probably be easier to take the locking-bar to a friendly garage or blacksmith to have it extended.

fourteen

Miscellaneous matters

WARPED TOPS AND STILES

Warping is arguably the most difficult problem to resolve, and should only be tackled if it is very unsightly or if it interferes with the operation of a door or drawer etc.

Let us first tackle the problem of a table top or panel. It is of course preferable to do as little as possible, so the first thing to try is to place the offending piece of wood over a wet surface, with the bow uppermost. A good idea is to wet an area of concrete and place the top over it, with some support along the edges and a little weight in the middle. It should be left in this way until the warp is slightly over-corrected. It may be necessary to leave the top in this position for two or three days, but it must be checked at regular intervals to make sure that all is well.

If this method does not work and the warp really does have to be taken out, then it may be necessary to cut a series of grooves in the underside of the top. These grooves will have to be at least three-quarters the depth of the top. How close together the grooves are cut will depend on the severity of the warp. The greater the degree of warp the closer together the grooves, and generally speaking lots of narrow grooves are better than a few wide ones. Cramp the top flat on a piece of blockboard or the like, with the grooves uppermost. Fill the grooves with wooden fillets of the same type of wood. The fillets should be a nice snug fit – it is important that they fill the groove all the way to the bottom. When the glue is dry the waste wood can be planed off and the surface coloured so that the fillets are not too obvious. This repair is a very drastic measure and has many limitations. It cannot be used if both top and bottom surfaces show; even if they don't, this repair will have a detrimental effect on the value of the piece, and should only be used if the warp is very bad. If the warped top is veneered it may in some cases be a better option to lift the veneer and relay it on a new top. (See Chapter 8.)

WOODWORM

Woodworm! How people cringe at the very name. Indeed, woodworm is both very

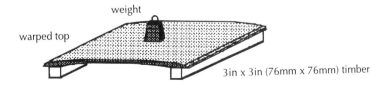

weight

warped top

3in x 3in (76mm x 76mm) timber

area of concrete

Fig. 101 Correcting a warped table top or panel.

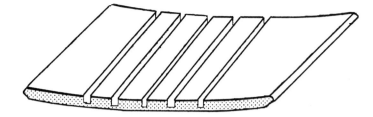

grooves cut in underside of top

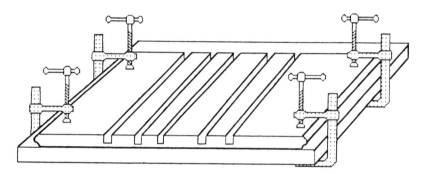

top cramped flat, ready for fillets to be glued in

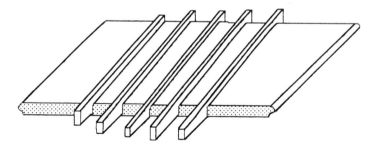

fillets glued in place and cramps removed when the glue is dry

Fig. 102 Correcting warping by cutting grooves.

harmful and very unsightly. Mahogany, however, is unaffected by worm – one of the main reasons it took over from oak and walnut as the main furniture wood around 1720.

The furniture beetle and the death-watch beetle are both woodworm. The death-watch beetle is much the larger of the two, but as it does not normally attack furniture it is of no interest to us here, although the life cycles of the two pests are basically the same.

The beetle lays its eggs in a crevice or slightly open joint, usually around May or June, and the larva or grub emerges after about three weeks. The grub tunnels into the wood where it remains for anything up to two years until fully grown. At this time it will make its way near to the surface of the wood, where it changes from the larva to the pupal stage. After a while it emerges from its chrysalis and bores its way out through the remaining layer of wood. It is these emergence or flight holes that one sees as evidence of woodworm. The adult beetle will then fly, usually not very far, and lay its eggs so the cycle can start again.

Woodworm can be killed by treating with any of the more common woodworm killers. The woodworm killer can be brushed onto the surface of unpolished timber and allowed to soak in. However, on polished surfaces it will have to be injected into the flight holes. It is best done in every hole under pressure with some kind of injector. This is best done using the type of nozzle which seals the hole while it is being injected.

Although the beetle itself can be fairly easily despatched, the flight holes are quite another problem. If there are not too many of the holes then they can either be ignored, or filled with wax stopper, but if they are numerous enough to have weakened the structure, then it is possible that parts of the cabinet will have to be replaced. If this is the case, every effort must be made to preserve as much of the original as possible. For example, although a veneered rail may be badly wormed and have to be changed, it is possible that the veneer itself may not have too many holes in it, and can be saved.

STOPPERS

A variety of proprietary stoppers can be purchased in tins. They come in different colours and they are useful if a large number of cracks or holes have to be stopped in. Most stoppers of this type have to be left proud of the surface and are then sanded down when dry. For this reason they can only be used if the surface is to be repolished. Check to see if they will take stain. Always try them out on a piece of waste timber first, so that you can see how the colour is affected when you polish it over.

POLISHER'S PUTTY

Polisher's putty is made from a mixture of French polish, whiting and dry colouring powders. These are mixed up to a creamy paste. This is a good stopper to use for small cracks, on table tops or surfaces that are going to be French polished. The stopper is left proud of the surface and sanded down when dry. It is as well to remember, when making up this type of stopper, that the colour lightens on drying, so it should be made darker than required.

WAX STOPPER OR BEAUMONTAGE

To make a wax stopper, melt a quantity of beeswax and mix with dry colouring powder to the desired colour. Add a few drops of white polishing oil and a small pinch of resin. Mix thoroughly and then turn out onto a cold surface and allow to dry. When dry, the stopper should be hard to the touch but should become pliable when kneaded between the fingers or slightly warmed. If the stopper is brittle when dry, it should be melted down and a little more oil added. If, however, the stopper does not go hard enough when dry, then more resin should be added. This wax stopper is ideal for small holes and cracks and is used on polished surfaces. It is pushed into the hole to be filled using the fingers or a piece of soft wood, and any excess is then rubbed off with a waxy rag.

STOPPER FOR USE UNDER VENEER

If you are about to veneer a surface that has a split or indentation, it can be filled with a stopper made up of whiting and scotch glue. This stopper has to be left slightly proud of the surface, cleaned down dry and then prepared with the toothing plane just as the rest of the surface.

REMOVING STAINS

Basically there are two types of stain: that which can be dealt with without removing the polish and that which cannot. Sometimes, with light alcohol or water stains and sometimes even with light scratches, sanding with fine flour paper and then rewaxing or lightly repolishing will be sufficient to remove the problem, but with deeper stains and with most ink stains the polish has to be removed. Sometimes, if you are lucky, the stain will be removed with the polish. If it is not, then other measures will have to be employed. As a rule of thumb, if the mark is light in colour then the chances are it is only in the polish. If the mark is dark it may be that it is in the wood itself, and the polish will certainly have to be removed if the stain is to be dealt with.

After removing the polish the first thing to do is to try a little household bleach applied with the end of a piece of tapered wood. Be careful to apply the bleach only to the stain, otherwise you could end up with a white line around the edge of your mark. If this does not work, the next thing to try would be 100-volume hydrogen peroxide. This will remove almost any stain I have come across, but please be careful with it. It is not the sort of thing that you want to get on your bare skin. This is also applied with the end of a piece of tapered wood and, again, you have to be careful to apply the bleach only to the mark and make sure that it does not creep over the edges. If even this fails, it is possible to make up a bleach with eight parts 100-volume hydrogen peroxide and one part 880 ammonia. This is a very strong bleach and great care must be taken not to get it on the skin or in the eyes. The bleach should be disposed of with a quantity of water immediately after use. Once the stain has been successfully removed it will be necessary to treat the area with water to remove all traces of the bleaching agent.

STAINS FROM GREASE OR FAT

Sometimes grease and fat stains can be removed by placing a piece of blotting paper over them and applying a little heat with a warm iron.

BURNS

Burns are not stains, and the only way they can be removed, other than simply colouring them out, is by scraping and sanding or cutting out the affected area.

CLEANING BRASS MOUNTS

Brass mounts on antique furniture should be cleaned only with a duster or soft brush while they are in place. If they need to be cleaned more thoroughly, they should be removed from the piece of furniture. Always check carefully, before cleaning, that the mounts have not been gilded, as most cleaning materials are abrasive and will eventually remove any gilding. If gilding is present it should only be necessary to clean with warm soapy water.

CLEANING TORTOISESHELL

Tortoiseshell is best cleaned with warm soapy water and then dried with a chamois leather. If any repairs have to be done you should be aware of two things: first, that tortoiseshell becomes pliable when placed in boiling water. If you want to shape a piece, cut a piece of wood to the required shape and form the shell to it as soon as it is removed from the water. The tortoise-shell will have to be held in position while it dries. Secondly, tortoiseshell can be welded together. Clean and scrape the surfaces to be welded. Contrive some device to hold them together and apply heat. The surfaces must be held together until they have cooled.

MARBLE REPAIRS

Broken marble is easily glued together with modern two-part epoxy resin such as araldite. Make sure that both edges to be joined are clean, and spread a thin coat of adhesive on both. If you are joining two large pieces, such as two halves of a top, it is a good idea to hold them together with cramps until the glue is dry. Araldite also makes an excellent stopper for marble – you can either mix it with some dry colouring powders, or you can scrape some marble powder off the underside of the marble you are joining. If filling holes in white marble, mixing the adhesive with talc gives good results. Marble can be lightly burnished with fine wet-and-dry paper.

CHAPTER

fifteen

Cane seating

The following tools are essential for completing all the jobs encountered when repairing cane seating:

A sharp penknife or craft knife
A small hammer
Scissors
A long bradawl
A metal rod or clearing tool
Plastic golf tees

THE CANE

Cane, or rattan, is grown in the Eastern tropics and it is only the inner bark that is stripped off and cut into various widths for seat caning. The width sizes are from No. 1, which is the narrowest to No. 6, which is about 6mm in width. Normally you might use a No. 3 cane for, say, a bedroom chair, but it depends really on the spacing of the holes. Most chairs will have holes that are about 12 to 14mm apart at the centres, but if they are wider apart than that it would be worth considering using a wider cane. In most cases there will probably be at least some of the original cane left to go by, even if the chair has since been upholstered.

The cane is best used when damp, so put a few lengths into a bucket of tepid water for five minutes and then keep them wrapped in a damp towel, taking one out for use as required.

REMOVING THE OLD CANE

The first step is to clean out all the old holes. After cutting through the cane near the inside of the seat frame, push a steel rod or six inch nail with a flattened point through the holes. On very rare occasions it will be necessary to drill the hole out, but do this only as a last resort.

THE SIX WAYS PATTERN

1. Determine which is the centre hole on both the back and front rails of the seat. Then take the first length of cane and

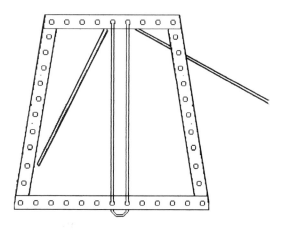

Fig 103 (a)   Stage one: the first cane.

Each time you go through a hole it is a good idea to peg it while you thread the next one so that the cane does not slip back and sag, but the peg can be moved along each time as the work progresses, so that each length you are dealing with need have only two pegs at any one time. Now go through the whole process again with the end of the cane that was under the seat rail, again ensuring that all finished ends are underneath the seat and all pegs are above. Make sure that when you start a new piece of cane, you start it on the opposite seat rail from the one you finished the last piece on. Continue until all holes in the back seat rail have cane running through them, *except for the corner holes*, which will be done later.

Where the seat has more holes in the front seat rail than the back, these will have the cane running from them to a hole in the side rail of the seat, to ensure that the lines of cane are kept parallel. It is very important to ensure that the right side of the cane is uppermost, even under the seat.

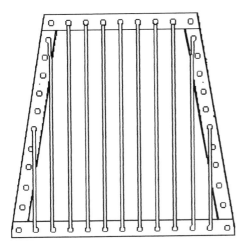

Fig 103(b)   Stage one completed.

thread it down through the hole for about half its length and secure it in position with a golf tee. Take hold of the section that is on top of the seat first, and thread it down through the centre hole in the front seat rail. Take care that you do not get the cane twisted by running your fingers along the full length of the cane, keeping the correct side uppermost all the time. Thread this end of the cane up through the hole next to it on the right or left whichever you prefer, and again, make sure the cane is not twisted. Now take the cane back to the corresponding hole in the back rail and thread it down through that one and up through the next one along and back again to the front. Continue in this way until you reach the end of the cane, or until you no longer have enough length to reach the other rail. Peg this end with a golf tee, and ensure that all ends are underneath the seat frame.

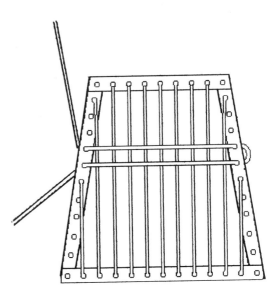

Fig 104   Stage two.

2. Repeat this process exactly the same way as before, working from one side seat rail to the other, on top of stage one, and once again leaving the corner holes free.

3. Repeat the first process again, now working on top of stage two. As you proceed try to ensure that the step three cane lies to the side of the first row and not over the top of it, as this is very important to the success of the finished seat.

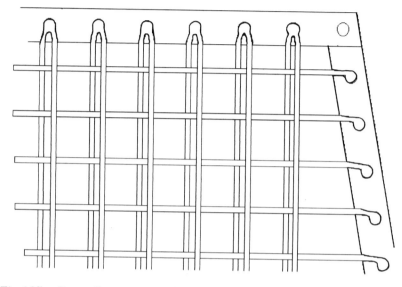

Fig 105   Stage three goes over the top of stage two.

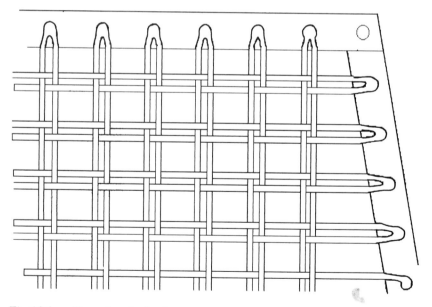

Fig 106   Stage four is the first cane to be weaved and goes over the first and under the second cane in each pair.

4. It is important to get this stage correct or the previous lines will not work out correctly. Start a new piece of cane on the right side rail, one hole up from the corner. Take this cane across to the other side rail, weaving it over the first and under the second of each of the vertical canes and just below or to the front of the cane of stage two. When doing this it is best to thread the cane through two or three vertical pairs of canes and pull it straight rather than try to go across the whole width of the seat in one go, as this would put undue strain on the vertical canes. Whilst weaving this stage you can ensure that, as you go, stage three lies to the side of stage one and this will keep it in place.

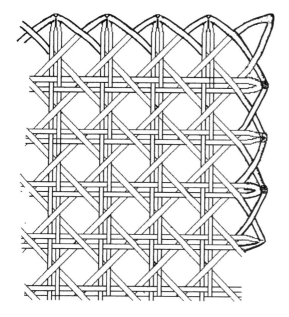

Fig 107 Stage five is the diagonal. From right to left go over the verticals and under the horizontals. From left to right go under the verticals and over the horizontals.

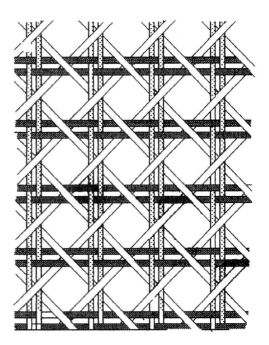

Fig 108 The diagonal from right to left goes under the horizontal pair, because the second cane of the vertical pair also goes under. This allows the cane to lie flat and wear less quickly.

5. This is your first diagonal and begins from the rear right hand side. Feel the end of the cane down through the back right corner hole until you have about 4in of cane under the seat. *This is the first time that this hole has been used.* Peg this in position with a tee, and proceed to weave the long end across to the left hand side of the seat, going over the vertical pairs and under the horizontal pairs of canes. This cane will probably not end up at the opposite corner, but somewhere on the left side rail, but in any case you must keep a true diagonal no matter where it comes out. When you get to the left side, thread the cane down through whichever hole it comes to and then up through the next hole to the back of the seat. Then work your way back to the other side following the first diagonal and keeping parallel to it.

Complete the top left hand triangle of the seat in this way, weaving over the verticals and under the horizontals. When this is completed, thread another cane down through the back right corner hole and complete the bottom right triangle of the seat in the same manner as the top left, weaving the diagonal cane over the vertical and under the horizontal. When this is completed you must go through the whole operation again, this time starting from the back left corner hole and working across to

the right. However, when working from left to right with the diagonals you must go *under* the verticals and *over* the horizontals. This is the opposite of the process when you worked from right to left. This is very important as otherwise the cane will wear more quickly because it does not lie so flat, as can be seen from Fig. 108. It is important to make sure that a diagonal goes into every hole in both the front and back seat rails. This may mean that adjustments have to be made on the sides and it is quite acceptable to miss a hole on the side rail, or to put in an extra cane.

FINISHING OFF

To finish off the seat on an antique chair it is necessary to peg every hole. The pegs are made from the round centre cane and must be cut into lengths a little shorter than the depth of the seat frame. Hammer a peg into each hole, at first with a small hammer but when you get near to the seat it will be best to use the steel rod used earlier as a punch so that you do not damage the polish with the hammer. Once the holes have been pegged all that remains to be done is to cut off all the short lengths of cane from under the seat.

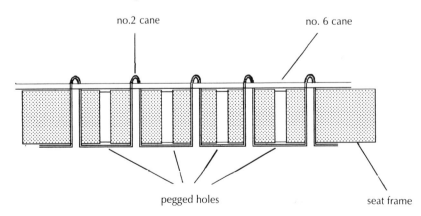

Fig 109 Finishing off.

On some seats you will find that the holes have been covered with a larger cane running around the edge of the frame, and the technique for doing this is as follows. Every other hole will need to be pegged leaving the corner holes unpegged. If you have an even number of holes, leaving two holes together that are either pegged or unpegged, make sure that these are in the centre of the rail. Stick some masking tape on the seat rail so that you can put a mark by the holes that are to be pegged. Any cane ends underneath the seat that are in non-pegged holes will need to be threaded up into a pegged hole. You can now peg all the marked holes as described above. In those holes that have cane ends threaded back up, take care not to push the ends back out as you peg the hole. Cut off all excess cane ends.

Next take a length of No. 2 cane and thread it down through the first open hole down from the back right corner of the frame. Then take it back up through the corner hole leaving an end of about 2in, which you lay flat covering the holes on the side rail. Take a length of No. 6 and taper one end to a point. Thread this end down into the corner hole and lay it over the end of the No. 2 cane. Peg the corner hole with a golf tee. Thread the No. 2 cane back down the same hole that it came up, but over the No. 6 cane, thus holding it firmly in place over the pegged hole. Feed the No. 2 cane up through the next open hole, over the No. 6 cane and back down again, and continue in this way until you reach the corner. At the corner you will have to cut the No. 6 cane just long enough to be able to taper the end and then thread into the corner hole. The end of the No. 2 cane can be taken across the corner and be threaded up through the first open hole in the front rail. Take another piece of No. 6 cane, taper the end as before and push it into the front right corner hole at right angles to the first No. 6 cane. Lie this cane over the holes in the front rail and hold it

in position with the No. 2 cane as before, after first permanently pegging the corner hole. When you have returned to the starting hole, thread the last end in and peg the hole. This last peg should be the only peg that will show on the completed seat.

Once completed the seat may need to be coloured to match some other part of the piece of furniture. It is possible to colour the cane with a water stain; usually a little Vandyke stain mixed so that it is not too dark will do the trick. Apply the stain with a brush as this is the only way to ensure you get good coverage where the canes cross. Start underneath, making sure you get well into the corners, and then cover the top of the seat. When you are sure that all has been covered wipe off the excess stain with a cloth, once again starting underneath and finishing on top. Allow the cane to dry and seal the colour with a coat of shellac. This will also add to the antique look of the new cane.

CONCEALED HOLES

If the back or arms of a chair are caned, the holes at the back or at the sides of the arms look very unsightly. To overcome this the holes are drilled in grooves or channels in the frame, which are filled with wooden fillets when the caning has been completed. Unfortunately these fillets have to be removed in order to recane, and as they are glued in place and polished over to match the frame, they cannot be removed without damage. The trick is in keeping the damage to a minimum. If you have a good edge to show where the fillets are, you can use a cutting gauge to scribe into the polish and the side of the fillets so that the edge will not break away when you chop out the fillet. If you do not have such an edge then you must very carefully follow the line of the fillet with a sharp chisel or craft knife. When you have scribed the edge of the fillet, take a sharp mortise chisel and chop out the fillet, taking care not to break the edge of the groove.

Clean out the holes and recane as described, and then cut and fit matching fillets into the grooves. The fillets are glued in place and cleaned down flush with the surface when dry, using firstly a plane and then a cabinet scrape. Stain and polish the fillets to match. When you have built up polish on the new fillets by the use of a polishing mop, make up a rubber for French polishing. Fill it with very dilute shellac and go over the new fillets and the sides of the frame with the mixture, and you should be able to blend in the old and new polish. If you can match the colour well the end result should be quite acceptable.

Professional Bodies

LAPADA   London and Provincial Antique Dealers Association
BADA   British Antique Dealers Association
BAFRA   The British Antique Furniture Restorers Association

Membership of BAFRA is only open to artist craftsmen who have been engaged in full-time restoration for a minimum of five years. Candidates for BAFRA Membership are required to provide satisfactory references and are assessed by an Examiner appointed by the Executive Committee. Candidates are assessed on the level and diversity of their skills, their knowledge of antique furniture and its history and also on their integrity as conservators. Their studio/workshops are assessed and they must satisfy the need for the highest level of professional standards. The Examiner's finding are then presented to the Executive Committee for approval. Only individual artist craftsmen may become members of BAFRA. Companies, Trade Associations and Guilds are not admitted.

Index

INDEX